ARMAGEDDON,

OIL

AND

TERROR

What the Bible says about the future

TYNDALE HOUSE PUBLISHERS, INC., CAROL STREAM, ILLINOIS

ARMAGEDDON, OIL AND TERROR

WHAT THE BIBLE SAYS ABOUT THE FUTURE

JOHN F. WALVOORD
with MARK HITCHCOCK

Visit Tyndale's exciting Web site at www.tyndale.com

Visit the author's Web site at www.walvoord.com

TYNDALE and Tyndale's quill logo are registered trademarks of Tyndale House Publishers, Inc.

Armageddon, Oil, and Terror: What the Bible Says about the Future

Designed by Stephen Vosloo

Previously published in 1974 and 1990 as *Armageddon, Oil and the Middle East Crisis* by Zondervan under ISBN 0-310-53921-8.

First published as *Armageddon, Oil, and Terror* by Tyndale House Publishers, Inc., in 2007.

Library of Congress Cataloging-in-Publication Data

Walvoord, John F.
  Armageddon, oil, and terror: what the Bible says about the future / John F. Walvoord with Mark Hitchcock.
    p. cm.
  Rev. ed. of Armageddon, oil, and the Middle East crisis. Rev. ed. c1990.
  Includes bibliographical references.
  ISBN-13: 978-1-4143-1610-9 (hc: alk. paper)
  ISBN-10: 1-4143-1610-0 (hc : alk. paper)
  ISBN-13: 978-1-4143-1582-9 (sc : alk. paper)
  ISBN-10: 1-4143-1582-1 (sc : alk. paper)
  1. Bible—Prophecies. 2. Middle East—Politics and government—1945- 3. World politics—1945-4. Armageddon.
5. Civilization, Western. 6. Petroleum industry and trade—Middle East. I. Hitchcock, Mark.
II. Walvoord, John F. Armageddon, oil, and the Middle East crisis. III. Title
  BS649.N45 W34 2007
  236'.9—dc22   2006102644

Printed in the United States of America

13 12 11 10 09 08 07
 7 6 5 4 3 2 1

Contents

Preface

DR. JOHN F. WALVOORD WAS NOT A PROPHET. But most would agree that he knew more about the prophecies of the Bible than any man who lived in the last century. During his long life he dedicated himself to the study of biblical prophecy in the original languages and the cultural context of the day in which the prophets spoke.

Dr. Walvoord was widely recognized as the "dean" of Bible prophecy scholars and teachers in the twentieth century. He taught thousands of seminary students at Dallas Theological Seminary, wrote and contributed to more than thirty books, traveled extensively, and spoke to audiences around the world. His contribution to the church's understanding of what the Bible says will happen in the end times is inestimable.

In the late 1930s Dr. Walvoord declared that the Jews would return to their ancient homeland and Israel would become a new and powerful Jewish state. In the mid-1940s he repeatedly wrote that the Jews would be restored to Israel.[1] His interpretation of prophecy led him to believe that Israel had to become a state amid its enemies—no matter what the odds. He insisted Israel had to be established and survive or end-time prophecies could not be fulfilled. His literal interpretation proved to be correct. The state of Israel was established in 1948. And Israel has miraculously survived one attack after another.

Over a period of five decades, Dr. Walvoord wrote numerous books and articles on topics related to the end times. Time and time again, he sketched out lists of end-time events that became headlines years after he put them in writing. While all of his works are important and valuable, in terms of popular impact, one of his books stands alone: *Armageddon, Oil and the Middle East Crisis.*

This classic book on end-time prophecy was originally published in 1974. The outline of events he had taught throughout the previous decades came alive in the wake of the 1973 Yom Kippur War in Israel and the subsequent Arab oil embargo against the United States. Dr. Walvoord seized upon the interest in world events at that time as a unique opportunity to show how these events pointed toward the Bible's scenario for the end times.

The book, with very minor revision, was rereleased sixteen years later in 1990 in light of the Persian Gulf War. Dr. Walvoord often commented how even after sixteen years the prophetic interpretations in the book remained rock solid and required no major changes. The revised book hit the *New York Times* best-seller list and sold millions of copies. It has been translated into ten languages and is still studied throughout the world.

Dr. Walvoord was perhaps less shocked by the events that occurred on September 11, 2001, than many of his contemporaries. He had predicted the rise of Islamic terrorism. He had predicted that terrorism and access to oil would be at the center of end-time events that would rock the world.

Before his death on December 20, 2002, Dr. Walvoord told many of his students that he believed the rise of militant Islam and the war on terror might be the final piece to the prophetic puzzle. It does seem that a kind of prophetic "shift of gears" occurred on 9/11 when world attention was riveted on the Middle East.

Our post-9/11 world seems to be on a downhill collision course. Terrorism has made the world increasingly dangerous. Some say we are already in World War III. Security, safety, and peace are the top priorities on everyone's agenda. There is an almost desperate yearning for peace and safety. Israel's struggle with Hamas and Hezbollah is now a centerpiece in the war on terror, which could lead to a nuclear confrontation between Israel and Iran. Add to all this the fact that the world's thirst for Middle Eastern oil shows no signs of diminishing.

The providential presence of crude oil in the Middle East and record prices for this resource have riveted world attention on the Middle East. The security and continued prosperity of the United States and Western Europe are vitally linked to the uninterrupted flow of Middle Eastern oil.

Much has transpired in the sixteen-plus years since the release of the second version of Dr. Walvoord's classic best seller. That is why the two of us—one his son, the other his student—have collaborated to revise and update this Bible prophecy classic for another generation. It reveals once again the timeless echo of Bible prophecy as history appears to move rapidly to the last events predicted to occur before the end of the age. Once again, it points another generation of readers to the relationship between prophecies in the Bible and the headlines and events we see around us.

Great care has been taken not to change any of the core material or views of Dr. Walvoord, and some additional material has been drawn from his other works and conversations during the last two years of his life. As you can see, the original title has been changed to reflect Dr. Walvoord's belief that terrorism is an essential element that is setting the stage for the end-time scenario presented in Scripture. In chapter 1 we discuss a biblical view of prophecy. In each of the next twelve chapters, we examine a specific event—either occurring now or that will unfold in the months and years ahead—that points to the end times. In chapters 14 and 15, we explain why believers in Christ can have hope, even during today's tumultuous times.

Whether you have read Dr. Walvoord's original work and are anxious to read this update or are totally new to this material, we invite you to examine for yourself the incredible correspondence between events in our world today and God's prophetic outline found in Scripture.

—John E. Walvoord

—Mark Hitchcock

CHAPTER 1

WHY PROPHECY?

It's very difficult to prophesy, especially about the future.
CHINESE PROVERB

My interest is in the future, because I'm going
to spend the rest of my life there.
CHARLES F. KETTERING

HAVE YOU EVER DRIVEN DOWN a strange dark road in a blinding rainstorm? Every minute you wish you could see beyond the edge of the headlights to see what's ahead. If only you could know what was coming next—could intuitively know what's out there or predict what you'll find at the next bend in the road. We long to see ahead, to know, perhaps to avert disaster.

Can someone see what's ahead by intuition or a special gift? Can a prophet know the future because the path of our lives is part of a larger drama scripted ahead of time? This is what the prophets of the Bible claim. Can we know where we are in that pattern of events foretold by prophets, written in Scripture, or seen in apocalyptic visions of the future? That is what we'll explore in this book.

In the uncertain storm of the days in which we live, all of us yearn to see beyond the headlights—but can we?

THE TIME BOMB IN OUR POCKET

The terrorist bomb on a bus in Israel has jumped into everyman's life— the World Trade Center, the Pentagon, a subway in London, a train in Madrid, a hotel in paradise. No one is safe anywhere.

Four planes are hijacked. The World Trade Center is destroyed and the Pentagon attacked. The entire United States economy is thrown into a recession.

Hurricane Katrina hits the coast. Refineries stop. Ports are blocked. The price of gas soars. Oil companies report record profits. The economic cement of our lives is not cement at all.

These recent events have underscored a reality most Americans would rather ignore: We have vulnerabilities. One of the greatest is our dependence on foreign oil. The wheels of transportation that make capitalism possible depend on this oil—gas, diesel fuel, high-octane jet fuel. If the wheels stop, the economy will shatter. The supply line stretches across the world to Saudi Arabia, Iraq, Iran, and the Middle East.

New industrial nations are exploding. The rocket of economic growth in China and throughout Asia demands more and more oil. The world barely has enough to supply present demand. The clash of economic engines demands more oil when supplies are nearing the breaking point. In this decade, economic growth alone will cause an "oil break point."

In 2001, Osama bin Laden plotted to overthrow the monarchy in Saudi Arabia and take over the oil the West needs so desperately. Then he could demand any price. Demand anything.[1] In 2006, terrorists attempted to attack the heart of the Saudi Arabian oil and gas industry, the Abqaiq processing facility. Al-Qaeda claimed responsibility for the failed attack. The *New York Times* called it the first attack on Saudi Arabia's oil infrastructure.[2] In one day the story disappeared from the news.

Do these events signal what the future holds? What will happen when Islamic terrorists are willing to ignite chaos in the Middle East to destroy the Great Satan of the West? Is it possible to protect every wellhead, pipeline, processing facility, and tanker? Who will stop the sabotage, the trucks laden with explosives, the handheld rockets, the dirty bombs?

Terrorism exposes another vulnerability. The terrorist arsenal has been building for decades. Iran has purchased and supplied Russian and Chinese weaponry, which has passed through Syria into Lebanon. Before the Thirty-Four-Day War between Israel and Hezbollah in the summer of 2006, the militant organization's arsenal included approximately 13,000 rockets and medium-range missiles. Israel was surprised at the state-of-the-art weapons used by the terrorist organization. During that one clash, Hezbollah fired approximately 4,000 short- and medium-range missiles into northern Israel.

Many still believe that weapons and high explosives stored in Iraq were carried out by the truckload before American troops arrived in March 2003—and that much of these are returning in the hands of terrorists. Tons of sophisticated explosives from a wide variety of sources are now in the hands of terrorists around the globe.

Missiles, nuclear warheads, and enriched uranium from the former Soviet Union have been bought and sold around the world to the highest bidder. In the late 1980s Abdul Qadeer Khan, the renegade Pakistani nuclear engineer, sold uranium enrichment technology to Libya, North Korea, and Iran. Although Libya has given up its nuclear program, it is now clear that both Iran and North Korea have used these designs to further their nuclear programs. North Korea has the bomb and is working to perfect the means to deliver a nuclear warhead as far as the United States.[3] Public statements by Iranian president Mahmoud Ahmadinejad have led intelligence sources to believe that Iran will be able to construct powerful atomic bombs in the very near future.

Iran is hotly pursuing its nuclear program and has publicly declared its intent to obliterate Israel. Iran is fully aware that Israel might launch a preemptive strike on its nuclear production facilities, and it has financed and provided training for Hezbollah to amass thousands of rockets and build a terrorist army. In the summer of 2006 Hezbollah proved it could mount a sizeable threat to Israel's security.

By arming a proxy army in Lebanon, Iran is adding another dangerous card to the game. If Israel orders an air strike against Iran, Iran can immediately order Hezbollah to strike northern Israel from the ground and with rockets from the air. Many believe it will be difficult for Israel to launch a sustained air war in both Iran and Lebanon at the same time. As Hezbollah continues to grow in Lebanon, how can Israel threaten Iran with air strikes when its northern cities are not secure?

What's the next move? Will the United States or Israel launch a preemptive strike against Iran? Will the Israeli-Arab conflict go nuclear? Will Iran unleash nuclear jihad?

While Iraq's program to develop chemical and biological weapons under Saddam Hussein was not as sophisticated or successful as early intelligence estimates indicated, much of what was started there is now in the hands of terrorist organizations. Chemical and biological weapons are being developed in every corner of the world. Terrorists around the world download the knowledge necessary to create biological agents every day from Web sites that supply the critical information. Chemical and bacteriological warfare may be as big a threat to large populations as nuclear devices or even conventional nuclear warheads.

THE IMPENDING CRISIS

The rapidly increasing tempo of change in modern life has given the entire world a sense of impending crisis. Oil and terror, the two greatest issues facing the world today, are both centralized in the same part of the world—the Middle East. Since the oil and the terrorists are in the same location, it's easy to envision terrorist attacks that could damage or interrupt world oil production. The world crises at the top of almost everyone's list are the war on terror and maintaining an uninterrupted flow of oil.

The Middle East became the center of attention during the Gulf War in 1990–1991 and made many wonder whether that conflict was to be the final war of prophetic fulfillment. Although it soon became clear that it was not Armageddon, the entire world focused on the tense situation in the Middle East. The invasions of Afghanistan in 2001 and Iraq in 2003 seem only to have added fuel to the terrorist fire. The Middle East is a powder keg that could explode at any time.

How long can world tensions be kept in check? How long can the struggle between the West and Islamic terrorism be kept from becoming a global bloodbath? The ingenuity of man has devised means of human destruction that would have seemed incredible to a previous generation. With terrorist tactics ranging from dirty bombs and suitcase-sized nuclear devices to anthrax and smallpox used as weapons of mass destruction (WMDs), the world appears to be moving toward a gigantic crisis. Can it be that the prophets of doom are right? Is the world racing toward Armageddon, the end of Western civilization?

THE VOICE OF THE PROPHETS

As alarming as these events are, they really are not surprising in light of the Bible's end-time prophecies. For centuries, people of religious faith have considered the message of true prophets to be God's revelation of His plan for human history. The Old Testament books record the lives and works of many great prophets—Moses, Isaiah, Jeremiah, Ezekiel, Daniel, Hosea, Joel, Micah, and others. These men predicted future events in vivid detail, including the rise and fall of every major world empire that left its mark on the Middle East. Some of their predictions came true within their lifetimes. Now it appears that many of their astounding prophecies could be fulfilled at any time.

Jesus Himself claimed to be a prophet and quoted from Moses, Isaiah, Daniel, and Jeremiah—many times adding interpretive comments and detailed predictions of His own. His words have been confirmed by the test of time. Jesus' prediction of the fall of Jerusalem (Luke 21:20-24) was so vivid that the early church in Jerusalem was able to escape almost certain destruction by fleeing the city before Titus destroyed it in AD 70. As then, so now, crucial predictions about Jerusalem and the nation of Israel are, in fact, the key to understanding a carefully predicted chain of events that will mark the last days of our civilization.

Jesus predicted the persecution of the church, the fall of Jerusalem with the destruction of the Temple, the scattering of the Jews into all nations, and the amazing survival and growth of the church. Along with the Old Testament prophets, He saw a time when Israel would be reestablished as a nation (see Matthew 19:28; Matthew 24:15-20; and Acts 1:6-7). All this has been realized in history. But He also warned those who understood the Old Testament prophets to watch Jerusalem and the Middle East for signs of the approaching end of world civilization, the end of the "period of the Gentiles," also referred to in some

The Period of the Gentiles

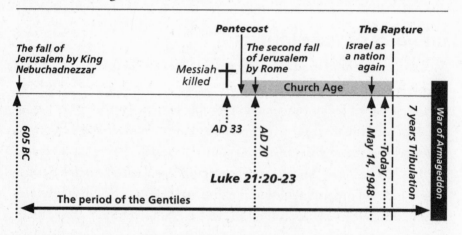

They will be killed by the sword or sent away as captives to all the nations of the world. And Jerusalem will be trampled down by the Gentiles until the period of the Gentiles comes to an end. (Luke 21:24)

translations as the times of the Gentiles. The Jews, He said, "will be killed by the sword or sent away as captives to all the nations of the world. And Jerusalem will be trampled down by the Gentiles until the period of the Gentiles comes to an end" (Luke 21:24).

Over five million Jews are now back in the land, the largest movement of Jews in history—far more than the two million who left Egypt for the Promised Land under Moses. Jerusalem, the city of dispute and negotiation, was won in 1967, only to become the object of a diplomatic tug-of-war. What is the future of the Holy City? If the period of the Gentiles is, in fact, nearing an end, what will happen next? What are the final events of world history as "the period of the Gentiles comes to an end"? Is there a sure word about tomorrow? Is this a word of hope or a warning of doom?

THE SEARCH FOR ANSWERS

Modern man is asking questions about the future as never before. They are solemn questions; they are searching questions. The Bible is certainly the best place to look for answers. Many of the biblical prophecies cited in this book are coming true before our very eyes. Even the most skeptical person can put these prophecies to the test by noting the literal, precise fulfillment of past prophecies.

For this reason, biblical prophecy is being discussed more than ever before. In these prophecies it is possible to probe for clues to find where we are in God's program and the predicted events that may occur in our lifetime. Prophecies, which in the past were sometimes brushed aside as incredible, are now being studied again.

The study of prophecy has been plagued by two extremes. The one extreme is to disregard prophecy or to interpret it in a nonliteral sense. About half of the prophecies in the Bible have been fulfilled. Studying these passages makes it clear that when prophecy in the Bible was fulfilled, it was fulfilled literally. The demonstrated pattern of fulfillment to date contradicts the skeptics' theories that prophecy should be considered metaphorically.

Another extreme, however, is to take prophecies out of context and interpret them to fit every headline. One prophecy isolated and out of context should not be used to interpret headlines or set dates for future events. The careful student of prophecy attempts to put all unfulfilled prophecies together into a chronology of events that is true to their literal meaning. Careful interpretation of prophecy reveals a chronology of events the Bible predicts will set the stage for the final act of world history.

As students of the Bible observe proper interpretation principles, they are becoming increasingly aware of a remarkable correspondence between the obvious trend of world events and what the Bible predicted millenia ago. In fact, 28 percent of the Bible was prophetic at the time it was written. Not surprisingly, then, people in all walks of life and of all religious faiths are asking the question—what does the Bible say the future holds?

NO VAGUE AND GENERAL PREDICTIONS

Unlike the self-proclaimed prophets of today, Jesus and the biblical prophets did not peddle vague and general predictions that could be adjusted to any situation. The prophecies recorded in the Bible are detailed and intricately interwoven. Although interpretation of minor points may vary, the overall picture is frighteningly clear.

The Bible does not simply speak of a final destructive world war but of a whole series of carefully timed events that are like signposts on the road to Armageddon.

Armageddon has come to describe anyone's worst fear of the end of the world. The prophets have described it more specifically as the final suicidal war of a desperate world struggle centered in the Middle East. It will be the final act in a terrifying series of events that are very much related to today's headlines. This final, history-shattering war will occur (1) on schedule, (2) at a specific time, and (3) in its predicted location.

The name *Armageddon* actually comes from a Hebrew word meaning "the Mount of Megiddo," a small mountain located in northern Israel at the end of a broad valley. This valley has been the scene of many military conflicts in the past and will be the focal point of this great future conflict.

The Bible clearly spells out the key events that will precede this last great conflict. The final countdown will involve years rather than days. Even before the countdown, the Bible predicts a number of preliminary moves, which will shape the political, economic, and religious climate necessary for end-time events. These preparatory steps are now falling into place in rapid succession. As these moves are completed, a more specific timetable of events can begin. The final countdown involves a brief period of preparation with the last seven years clearly delineated. The last half of these seven years will be three and a half years of unparalleled disaster and war, climaxing at Armageddon. Though we'll examine each of these events in greater detail later in the book, they are summarized below:

1. **Revival of the Roman Empire.** Prior to these last seven years, a group of ten leaders, or what we might call the "Group of Ten," will rise from Europe, as indicated by the ten horns of Daniel 7:7-8 and the similar description of the end-time government in Revelation 13:1. This alliance or confederacy of ten leaders and the nations they represent constitutes a revival of the Roman Empire and the beginning of the final stage of the fourth beast in Daniel 7.

   These countries will include European countries and possibly nations in western Asia and northern Africa. This Group of Ten will control the nations and geographic areas from the ancient Roman Empire. The Group of Ten will rise to power because the West will desperately need to guarantee the peace and security of the Middle East. This will temporarily be accomplished in a seven-year covenant of peace and protection with Israel. Without a forced peace, disruption of the West's oil supply and an escalation in terrorism will threaten to bring Western civilization to its knees.

2. **Israel's survival is threatened.** The reestablishment of the nation of Israel in the Middle East was necessary to start the Armageddon calendar. Almost since its birth, however, Israel has been threatened with extinction. Nonetheless, prophecy seems to indicate that Israel will not be destroyed by war. Instead, Israel will eventually be betrayed and forced to accept an outside settlement at the peace table. The Middle East oil blackmail and new economic and political alignments in the Middle East will eventually rob both the United States and Russia of a determining voice in the final settlement.

3. **True believers disappear.** The world will be traumatized by the fulfillment of what theologians call the rapture of the church—the sudden removal of every Christian from the world (1 Thessalonians 4:13-18). This will fulfill the promise of Christ to His disciples when He said, "I will come and get you, so that you will always be with me where I am" (John 14:3). At that time, Christians who have died will be resurrected, and every true Christian living in the world will be suddenly removed to heaven without experiencing death.

   The disappearance of millions of Christians will deepen the religious confusion, already evident in the current cultural obsession over the supernatural and mystical phenomena. The organized church with every true Christian removed will fall into the hands of political opportunists.

4. **Power is centralized in one man.** From the many negotiators and leaders involved in the Middle East, one new international leader will emerge from Europe to superimpose a peace settlement on Israel and the more militant Muslims and to assure the West's sup-

ply of oil. This will bring an era of false peace, a move toward disarmament, and a major push for a new world economic system. These first three and a half years will be the calm before the storm as the new leader consolidates his power.

The last three and a half years will include a series of almost inconceivable catastrophes. Just before this period begins, Russia and a group of Islamic allies will attempt a final bid for power in the Middle East, but their armies will be supernaturally destroyed (Ezekiel 38–39). The balance of power will swing decisively to the world's new strongman. As Satan's man of the hour, he will then attempt to destroy Israel, now disarmed and at peace. In the fashion of the Babylonian and Roman emperors, he will deify himself and command the worship of the world.

5. **A series of natural disasters shake the world's foundations.**
The world will begin to come apart at the seams—worse than any ecologist's nightmare. Acts of man, resulting in thousands of martyrs, and acts of God will combine to cause great disturbances in the world and universe. Stars will fall and planets will run off course, causing chaotic changes in climate (Revelation 6:12-14; 16:8-9). Unnatural heat and cold, flooding, and other disasters will wipe out much of the food production of the world (Revelation 6:6-8). Great famines will cause millions to perish (Matthew 24:7). Strange new epidemics will sweep the world, killing millions. As the period draws to a close, earthquakes will level the great cities of the world, and geological upheavals will cause mountains and islands to disappear in the seas (Revelation 16:17-21). Disaster after disaster will reduce the world population in the course of a few years to a fraction of its present billions.

6. **The march to Armageddon.** Topping even these disasters
will come a world war of unprecedented proportions. Hundreds of millions of men will be involved in a gigantic world power

11

struggle centered in the Holy Land (Revelation 16:13-16). The area will become the scene of the greatest war of history. Great armies from the south will pour into the battle arena (Daniel 11:40) and other great armies from the north will descend on Israel (Daniel 11:41). Climaxing the struggle will be millions of men from the Orient and China who will cross the Euphrates River and join the fray (Daniel 11:44; Revelation 9:13-16; 16:12). Locked in this deadly struggle, millions will perish in the greatest war of all history. This is what the Bible describes as Armageddon.

Before the war is finally resolved and the victor determined, Jesus Christ will come back in power and glory from heaven. His coming, accompanied by millions of angels and raptured Christians, is described in graphic terms in Revelation 19. Coming as the King of kings and judge of the world, He will destroy the contending armies and bring in His own kingdom of peace and righteousness on earth.

As incredible as these prophecies are, even now the world is moving toward these events. The nations are taking their predicted places. The escalating crisis in the Middle East is a buildup to the start of the Tribulation. Ancient prophecies are being fulfilled. The world is rushing toward Armageddon!

THE FINAL ACT

Sometimes life feels like entering a dark theater and realizing you are coming in near the end of a play with several acts. We didn't write it. We didn't ask to be thrust into the play. We can be certain this drama is nearing the last act. Even though we did not see the beginning we can look back and see the plot and direction of the play. But even then, how can we be sure when the next act will start?

The prophets talked a lot about the last act. All we can do is look for the events that set up the last act. If they occur now, we can be fairly certain the last act is just ahead. When the curtain comes down on this scene, will the next act be the last? To be sure, we need to know what will happen on the world stage to set up the last act. What are the events, the characters, and the plot that will bring the play of world history to its predicted climax? Will we be wise enough to see it coming? Will we be ready? In the coming chapters, we will examine some of the events that are either already unfolding or that we know will occur based on biblical prophecy. We'll examine the first event in chapter 2, which shines the prophetic spotlight squarely on the Middle East.

 See how today's headlines relate to this chapter at
http://www.prophecyhotline.com.

CHAPTER 2

OIL BECOMES THE ULTIMATE WEAPON

EVENT #1: The Middle East becomes the center of a desperate struggle for oil as demand exceeds supply, prices soar, and industrialized nations fight for economic survival.

Oil depletion is arguably the most serious crisis ever to face industrialized society.

PAUL ROBERTS, *THE END OF OIL*

When, and in precisely what form, we will experience the next great energy shock cannot be foreseen. Perhaps it will be triggered by a coup d'etat. . . . Or it might be a major act of terrorism, or a catastrophic climate event. Whatever the case, our existing energy system, already stretched to its limits, will not be able to absorb a major blow.

MICHAEL T. KLARE, *BLOOD AND OIL*

IMAGINE THE DAY THE PRICE of oil triples. The news of the hour may be a hurricane or earthquake that has wiped out ports and refineries, a terrorist attack on the energy infrastructure in Saudi Arabia, wells on fire in Iraq, the sinking of supertankers in the Strait of Hormuz, or a nuclear interchange in the Middle East.

Like the events of 9/11 or news of any disaster, people around the world watch in shock. Few who watch the initial news reports can imagine how one or two simple catastrophes will change the world forever. The real shock is not the event—it is the domino effect when the oil break point occurs.

Most people rush to the closest gas or petrol station. Some of these businesses have handwritten "sold out" signs on the pumps. Many have broken windows. Others have lines of cars and trucks blocks long. In the panic many people wait in line with tanks half full of gas. Gas containers disappear from stores. When people begin to hoard, it makes matters worse. Countries also begin to hoard. One by one the industrial powers of the world announce the need to build massive strategic petroleum reserves. New restrictions and taxes on energy immediately become a priority of every government.

Overnight, a black market in heating oil, gas, and diesel fuel springs up. People begin worrying about the next winter. How will they heat their homes? How can they afford higher utility bills? Will their savings last that long?

The economic effects on transportation are obvious. Commuters who depend on automobiles cannot get to work. Airlines cancel flights and apply for government subsidies. Truckers refuse to load freight until prices stabilize. Ports back up as the transportation chain breaks down. Ships with cargo form long lines at sea waiting to come into port.

Those who can get to their jobs face an uncertain future. Businesses and factories that use transportation to supply just-in-time inventory come to a halt. Even assembly lines that keep running cannot ship products and equipment to their customers.

People begin to hoard everything. Stores close when present inventories are wiped out. Governments call out the military to establish order.

Yes, these scenes are easy to imagine. It is difficult to know how the oil break point would affect you and your family. But it's too late to pretend it cannot happen. If the supply of oil—or the energy infrastructure that refines and distributes oil—hits the breaking point, the economy of the United States and other industrial giants will desta-bilize. Third World countries struggling for survival will be destroyed by a disruption in the price and availability of oil. The break point will come when demand suddenly exceeds supply. Oil futures on the com-modity markets will spike. Nations will rush to hoard more strategic reserves. The high cost of petroleum products alone will cause the wheels of Western economic growth to grind to a halt. The world will be changed forever on that day.

CRUDE AWAKENING

In the fall of 1973, a group of Arab nations staged a Pearl Harbor–like attack on Israel on Yom Kippur (Day of Atonement), the most holy day of Judaism. Israel was able to ward off the invaders with the sup-port of several Western nations and maintain control of the strategic Golan Heights in the north, territory that Egypt and Syria had hoped to capture.

One of the important results of the war in 1973 was the coming together of Arab nations as never before. Although the unity was mani-fested partially in the military conflict, it became increasingly evident that the Arab world's bid for power was going to be based on its control of the major oil resources. In a new show of unity, the Arab world, on October 17, 1973, reduced its production of oil below the previous norm and attempted to embargo nations that favored Israel, principally the United States and the Netherlands.

The price of oil quadrupled to twelve dollars a barrel. The grim prospect of having insufficient fuel for homes, industry, and the military sent shock waves around the world. Those who lived through that time can still remember the long, winding lines at gas stations and the result-ing panic. A new war was in progress, an economic war of tremendous implications. For the first time in centuries, the Middle East became a major consideration in every international event.

In the 1970s the rapid increase in consumption of energy through-out the world brought warnings of an impending crisis. By then, oil had proven to be cheaper and easier to use than coal. Much of the United States' electricity, especially in the East, depended upon energy derived from oil. Ecologists had opposed the use of coal, particularly the lower grades that were economically feasible, because of air pollution. At that time nuclear power was opposed by just about everyone.

The continued increase in automobile travel, especially in the United States, led to a rising demand for oil for which there was no suitable substitute. Any reduction in oil supplies would inevitably affect automobile travel and with it the total automobile industry. The prospect of limited supplies of gasoline threatened the lifestyle as well as the economic prosperity of the United States. Europe and Japan were even more dependent on oil from outside sources, and the threat of limited oil produced panic unprecedented since the days of World War I. A whole new alignment of international power was underway, and no one could accurately predict the future.

Fast-forward to the twenty-first century. The United States continues to consume more and more oil each year. Americans use about 21 million barrels of oil a day, or 25 percent of the oil produced in the world. If present trends continue, U.S. consumption is expected to rise to 27 million barrels a day by 2020, and U.S. oil demand will expand 34 percent by 2030.[1]

China's accelerating economy has an insatiable thirst for oil. World demand shows no signs of slowing, while supply and production have remained static. No new refinery has been built in the United States since 1976, meaning the nation cannot count on much growth in its domestic production of oil.

The razor-thin margin between world supply and demand became apparent in August 2005 when hurricanes Katrina and Rita hit the Gulf Coast and sent shock waves through the world oil market. For the first time, gas prices shot up thirty cents a gallon to a national average of over three dollars a gallon. In 2006, gas prices went above three dollars a gallon several times before settling down. When they did, oil dropped out of the news.

But crude oil is a finite resource, and the rate of consumption is continuing to rise dramatically. Even though experts estimate that there is a forty-year supply, calculated at current consumption rates, the supply of cheap oil is dwindling, and the United States is still dependent on imports from hostile and potentially unstable nations.

While opinions on the time line vary, experts agree that the world's addiction to oil is "hastening a day of reckoning."[2] World oil demand hit 86 million barrels a day in 2006 and continues to grow at about two million barrels a day every year. Peter Tertzakian, chief energy economist at a leading energy investment firm, puts this in perspective. "Sometime in 2006, mankind's thirst for oil will have crossed the milestone of 86 million barrels per day, which translates to a staggering one thousand barrels a second!"[3]

When will the world no longer have access to affordable oil? According to a report in *National Geographic*: "It could be 5 years from now or 30: No one knows for sure, and geologists and economists are embroiled in debate about just when the 'oil peak' will be upon us. But few doubt that it is coming. 'In our lifetime,' says 46-year-old economist Robert K. Kaufmann of Boston University, 'we will have to deal with a peak in the supply of cheap oil.' The peak will be a watershed moment, making the change from an increasing supply of cheap oil to a dwindling supply of expensive oil."[4]

The peak in oil production outside the Middle East has already happened, and some industry observers believe the worldwide oil production peak will happen in 2016.[5] By as soon as 2010, the pressure for world consumption will push toward 95 million barrels a day. If present trends continue unchecked, projected world oil consumption in 2020 could rise to about 120 million barrels a day—up 60 percent from 1999. But where will the oil come from, and at what price?

THE VITAL ROLE OF MIDDLE EAST OIL

On the basis of proven oil reserves, the Arab world is in a good position to control oil production and blackmail other nations. The Middle

Oil Reserves by Country

COUNTRY	PROVED RESERVES (BILLION BARRELS)
1. Saudi Arabia	266.8
2. Canada	178.8
3. Iran	132.5
4. Iraq	115.0
5. Kuwait	104.0
6. United Arab Emirates	97.8
7. Venezuela	79.7
8. Russia	60.0
9. Libya	39.1
10. Nigeria	35.9
11. United States	21.8
12. China	18.3
13. Qatar	15.2
14. Mexico	12.9
15. Algeria	11.4
World Total	**1,292.5**

SOURCE: U.S. Energy Information Administration, "World Proved Reserves of Oil and Natural Gas, Most Recent Estimates" (posted October 5, 2006), based on information from *Oil & Gas Journal*, January 1, 2006.

East/Persian Gulf has about 60 percent of the known oil reserves of the world lying beneath its desert sands.

In addition, the countries of the Middle East have sophisticated handling and processing facilities that have been developed by the major Western oil companies. In rapid succession these facilities were nationalized. A few national leaders now control not only a major portion of the world's oil reserves but some of the most advanced production and processing facilities in the world. Without a continued supply of Middle Eastern oil, the industrial giants of the West simply do not have the energy they need for industrial production, transportation, electricity, and heat.

Of all the nations of the world, the United States is the largest consumer of crude oil, using one-fourth (about 20 million barrels a day) of the total production of the world. Still, the United States has taken no decisive action in the face of Arab threats. The nation managed to survive the 1973 embargo through a variety of indirect maneuvers, including increased imports from Iran. It also has made no advances in curbing increasing demand for oil or creating public policy that will lead to energy self-sufficiency.

THE PROBLEM THAT WON'T GO AWAY

The crisis of 1973 is history, but what was a passing problem may soon draw the Western world into a confrontation from which there is no escape. When the Arab nations first demonstrated their control over the world's oil in 1973, their first step was to restrict oil output and delivery. The cutbacks were linked to a demand for Israel's complete withdrawal from all lands that it had occupied by war, including the restoration of Jerusalem, or at least a portion of it, to the Arabs. Led by King Faisal of Saudi Arabia, the Arabs threatened to restrict the shipment of oil to the entire world and embargo oil to selected nations like the United States. Along with the restrictions on the amount of oil delivered were shocking increases in the price of oil.

In short-term results, the Arab oil blackmail in 1973 proved that Europe, Japan, and the smaller emerging industrial nations were more vulnerable to political manipulation than the United States and Russia, and this scenario continues today. The impact in Europe was felt immediately, and citizens quickly turned down their thermostats and restricted their automobile use. As the price of oil went up, so did the prices of almost everything else.

Japan was forced to pay increasing billions for oil imports, resulting in a temporary decline in its economy and increasing inflation. Within a year the inflation rates doubled in many countries, including Italy, France, Belgium, and Great Britain. Great Britain braced itself for the worst economic days since the 1930s, muddling through until reduction of consumption and North Sea oil production began to solve some of Britain's economic woes.

But the price of Persian Gulf crude oil did not decrease after the crisis of 1973–1974. In retrospect the prices seem low by today's standards. But higher oil prices and the continued pressure for price increases began to quietly erode the economic stability of the Western world. The Arab oil blackmail had begun the fastest transfer of money in history. A few Middle Eastern countries were accumulating more wealth more quickly than even the conquistadors when they seized the gold of the Incas. And the final price would not be exacted in gold alone, but in the political and economic reshaping of the world.

Europe Hedges Its Bets

In reaction to the energy crisis in 1973, energy policy changed across Europe. The European community generally saw the need both to reduce consumption and to impose taxes on gasoline to raise significant revenue.

High taxes on gasoline limited consumption and encouraged use of public transportation and the development of alternative energy sources. France pursued a policy to use nuclear reactors to supply much of its electrical power. By 2007, conservation was a way of life in Europe, and the price per gallon of gas was more than twice the cost in the United States. Prices above six dollars a gallon were the rule, and increases caused much less concern than in the United States.

Countries with high taxes on gasoline include Japan, Great Britain, Norway, Poland, Turkey, and South Korea. This shift took more than two decades to accomplish. Gasoline in Brazil is still more expensive than in the United States, but nearly all of the country's 34,000 gas stations offer ethanol as a flex-fuel at attractive prices. One reason Brazil has been able to convert to ethanol so quickly is because it's an ideal geographical location for growing sugar cane, a much more energy-rich feeding stock than corn, which the United States uses for its ethanol production.[6]

Like the rest of the world, Europe still needs fossil fuels and cannot live without them. Because the price of fuel is set in dollars, the strength of the euro holds down the price of oil as long as prices do not rapidly escalate. But if the underlying cost of oil doubles or triples, most countries will be pushed to the edge of economic disaster.

The United States Bets on Cheap Oil

Immediately after the energy crisis in 1973, the entire world began to increase oil discovery and production with new determination. The rise in oil prices suddenly made costly exploration and production methods worth the risk. But moves toward stimulating increased production or extensive exploration soon faltered in the United States as politicians debated and disagreed over energy policy decisions. Self-sufficiency seemed only a political slogan.

The initial drilling boom in the mid-1970s, combined with prior discoveries in Prudhoe Bay, Alaska, lifted U.S. production only 4 percent from 1979 to 1985. Then production began falling again. In 1985 the United States imported less than 30 percent of its oil. In the mid-1990s imported oil broke the 50 percent mark for the first time. By 2005–2006, the number reached 60 percent.[7] The gap between oil consumption and production continues to widen. Clearly, the United

U.S. Dependence on Imported Oil

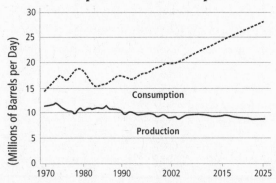

SOURCE: U.S. Energy Information Administration, "Annual Energy Outlook with Projections to 2025 - Market Trends - Oil and Natural Gas," Figure 99, http://www.eia.doe.gov/oiaf/archive/aeo04/gas.html (accessed December 12, 2006).

23

States is no longer one of the world's great producers of oil. To reverse the decline would require gigantic new reserves several times larger than Prudhoe Bay.

Of all the major oil importers, the United States had seemed to be in the best position to develop self-sufficiency at the time of the Arab oil embargo. Yet as time passed, the country was unable to move forward with a decisive energy program. The American public continued to believe that a cheap and plentiful supply of oil was their birthright.

As prices began to rise in 2005, the public outcry was directed at the oil companies, which seemed to be reaping exorbitantly high profits. ExxonMobil had a record $36.1 billion profit in 2005 and gave its chairman a $400 million retirement deal. It was estimated that 2006 profits for ExxonMobil would soar to about $40 billion.[8] As prices rose even more rapidly in 2006, however, that anger seemed aimed at the government.

That isn't surprising. When any major problem confronts a society, the first reaction is generally anger, resignation, and wishful thinking. It takes much longer to develop a society's will to change and embrace lifestyle changes. The price of oil was lowered by increases in production before and during the elections in 2006. The public outcry focused on the war and overlooked the issue of energy self-sufficiency. But the problems of oil and war are inextricably linked.

Breaking the dependence on foreign oil will not be easy—and may take decades. Increased exploration and development cannot solve the problem without painful conservation and a switch to alternative fuels.

THINKING OUTSIDE THE BARREL

In 2005 the United States consumed about seven billion barrels of oil and the equivalent of eleven billion barrels of oil in the form of coal, natural gas, uranium, and hydroelectric power. The United States is rich in coal—with the equivalent of one trillion barrels of oil.[9]

Uranium is abundantly available for nuclear power. Heavy oil sup-

Oil Consumption *(Barrels per Day)*

1. United States	20,030,000
2. European Union	14,590,000
3. China	6,391,000
4. Japan	5,578,000
5. Russia	2,800,000
6. Germany	2,677,000
7. India	2,320,000
8. Canada	2,300,000
9. South Korea	2,061,000
10. France	2,060,000
11. Italy	1,874,000
12. Saudi Arabia	1,775,000
13. Mexico	1,752,000
14. United Kingdom	1,722,000
15. Brazil	1,610,000
World Total	**80,100,000**

SOURCE: Central Intelligence Agency, *The World Factbook 2006*

plies in the form of tar sands in Alberta, Canada, far exceed the oil reserves of Saudi Arabia. But coal, uranium, or tar sands will not solve the immediate problem. Energy equivalence on paper is not gasoline in the tank.

The problem is America's continued dependence on light crude oil. Approximately 40 percent of the fuel the United States consumes is oil—used primarily for cars, trucks, trains, and airplanes. The nation consumes 43 percent of the world's motor gasoline. Without it, the transportation system of the entire U.S. economy would collapse. Addiction to this specific form of energy means that the United States cannot dodge the bullet if anything suddenly disrupts the supply of light crude oil from the Middle East.

Given the increasing volatility of the Middle East, the United States must carefully consider all possible alternatives. One of America's other primary sources of foreign oil is Venezuela, but prospects for a continuing, productive relationship are uncertain—at best. As Venezuela continues to struggle with its own political discontent, the South American country's president, Hugo Chavez, openly criticizes the "imperialist policies" of the United States. Now representing the Venezuelan-owned, mega-oil-producer Citgo, Chavez has traveled numerous times to Iran and is closely allied with Iranian president Mahmoud Ahmadinejad. Chavez has signed a series of energy accords with Iran, including a two-billion-dollar investment fund to finance special projects. If a regional conflict breaks out in the Middle East, particularly involving Iran, the danger looms that Venezuela will use oil as a weapon and carry out threats to cut off the United States' supply.

For decades visionaries have dreamed of hydrogen as the ultimate replacement for petroleum for cars and trucks. But this cannot happen without decades of research and development. It would mean new energy production, new cars, and entirely new fueling stations. Even a trillion dollar investment in a switch to hydrogen would take decades to implement.

A lead article in *Fortune* magazine on the future of fuel announced, "Stop dreaming about hydrogen. Ethanol is the answer to the energy dilemma. It's clean and green and runs in today's cars. And in a generation, it could replace gas."[10]

For transportation, biofuels are the most likely replacement for fossil fuels. Today's gas stations can handle a mix of up to 85 percent ethanol and 15 percent gasoline. "Flex-fuel" vehicles or "E85" vehicles would allow conventional automobiles to burn either gasoline, ethanol, or both. Ethanol produces less energy per gallon than gasoline—it takes about 30 percent more ethanol per mile than gasoline—but it's one answer to the United States' dependence on light crude oil. And ethanol could be delivered using the current infrastructure of gas stations across America.

But a rapid transition to use cornstarch ethanol for all transportation in America is simply not possible at current consumption levels. Some critics believe that producing fuel from crops consumes more energy than it produces. In 2006 American production of ethanol consumed 14 percent of the country's corn production while providing little relief from the country's dependence on fossil fuels.[11] To divert more of the country's food supply to ethanol would create serious shortages in the world food supply and still would not meet the demand. It takes eleven acres of land to grow enough corn to power one car with ethanol for one year (ten thousand miles). That's the same amount of land required to feed seven people for one year.

David Pimentel of Cornell University notes that if we decided to run all our cars on ethanol we would need to cover 97 percent of our land with corn. Of course, ethanol could be used simply to supplement our gasoline needs, not totally replace them. But it doesn't appear to be an immediate answer to the problem.[12] According to reporter Adam Wilmoth, "Some maintain that even if the entire grain production of the United States were converted to ethanol, it would only equate to a 16 percent reduction in petroleum usage."[13]

The position of the U.S. Energy Department is that the development of cellulose-based ethanol will be necessary to significantly cut our dependence on gasoline. Cellulose comes from the walls of plant cells and can be extracted from cornstalks, grasses, tree bark—things that are abundant and that would not disrupt the world's food supply. The U.S. Congress passed a comprehensive energy bill on July 29, 2005, that mandated the use of 250 million gallons of cellulosic ethanol a year by 2013. The engineering and production problems to do this have not yet been solved.

Can biofuels replace gasoline in time to prevent a major conflict in the Middle East? The 250 million gallons of ethanol mandated to be produced in 2013 would amount to less than the equivalent of two days supply of gasoline consumed in the United States.

The Natural Resources Defense Council has charted a future in which biofuels will slowly replace gasoline as technology makes transportation more efficient. The group advocates aggressive government investment in research, development, and deployment, noting that "the private sector is unlikely to invest on the scale or at the speed that we need if we are to wean ourselves from oil." [14]

Even if it does so, from 2010 to 2020 biofuels will replace only a fraction of the consumption of oil. It will still take from 2020 to 2035 to replace more than half of the petroleum used for transportation. The Department of Energy predicts that it will take until at least 2030 for ethanol to put a 30 percent dent in America's gasoline consumption. [15]

All the available research on alternative energy sources to replace gasoline comes to the same conclusion. *Fortune* says, "In a generation, it [ethanol] could replace gas." [16] It will take time—at least a decade, more likely two decades—and an extraordinary change in the U.S. culture to make this happen. Even at lower consumption rates, alternative energy sources for transportation for Great Britain and Europe will be equally difficult to achieve in a short time frame. The Council on Foreign Relations said that U.S. energy independence is impossible for "at least several decades" and "unachievable for the foreseeable future." [17] Until then, what happens in the Middle East may still throw the West into panic and cause severe economic hardship.

New energy sources to replace oil lost to natural disasters, terrorism, war, or a nuclear exchange in the Middle East are at least ten to twenty years away. For now, the West has no alternative but to defend its supply of oil at any cost.

That means, for the foreseeable future, oil will power the global economy. The question remains—does the United States have the will to reduce its dependence on foreign oil? Is it possible that America will allow its economic future to be destroyed by international events it cannot control?

In the first decade of the twenty-first century, dependence on Middle Eastern oil is increasing at the same time terrorism, the threat of nuclear weapons, and instability are rising in the Middle East. This volatile combination of terrorism, weapons of mass destruction, and the coming break point in oil supply is an explosive mix that could threaten to push the entire civilized world into chaos.

WHOM CAN ISRAEL TRUST?

From Israel's standpoint, the situation is decidedly an unhappy one. If the United States is weakened by a new energy crisis, will it continue its unilateral support of Israel?

How long will America continue to defend Israel's interests when the United States itself so desperately needs oil from the Persian Gulf? The nation became deeply committed to the defense of Saudi Arabia and Kuwait during the first Iraq war. The second Iraq war once again revealed the United States' determination to control events in the region. But can the military intervention of the United States really stop the disintegration of the balance of power in the region? With the growing problems in Iraq and Afghanistan, how long will the United States be willing to commit its military forces in the region? Will it have the political and economic will to stop the proliferation of nuclear weapons in hostile countries like Iran?

The Middle Eastern countries supply oil, but they also supply the money needed for industrial investment and to finance government deficits. They're awash in oil money. As purchasers of vast amounts of military hardware, machinery, and technology, they can choose to buy or not to buy from any particular country. These wealthy nations can choose to shift vast amounts of money from dollars to euros. They can invest in, or pull all their investments from, any country they choose. In terms of money alone, the other Arab countries and Iran have a vast amount of investable income that can be moved from bank to bank or country to country—which could play havoc with world currencies and world trade.

In long-term results, the Arab countries and Iran have been able to consolidate both wealth and power. The cost to the world, and especially to Israel, will not just be calculated in petrodollars. These new realities are forcing a closer relationship between key European countries and some of the most powerful countries in the Middle East. Russia has forged an economic and political alliance with Iran. China and India are becoming huge consumers of oil. China will deal with anyone, even outlaw states, that can supply its growing need for oil. The enormity of the coming energy crisis will seize the attention of the entire world.

THE UNITED STATES TO USE "ANY MEANS NECESSARY"

In the wake of the 1973 oil embargo and the 1979 Iranian hostage crisis, the Persian Gulf region rose to the very top of the U.S. security agenda—a place it has occupied ever since. President Jimmy Carter announced an important policy change in 1980. In his State of the Union address on January 23, 1980, he said that access to the Persian Gulf was a vital national interest. He declared that to protect that interest the United States was prepared to use "any means necessary, including military force." The policy became known as the Carter Doctrine.

In August 1990 President George H.W. Bush and defense secretary Dick Cheney put the Carter Doctrine into action. On August 2, 1990, Saddam Hussein sent Iraqi troops into neighboring Kuwait. This move immediately alarmed the United States over fear that Iraq might try to move into Saudi Arabia, thereby controlling almost half of the world's proven oil reserves (the total oil reserves of Iraq, Kuwait, and Saudi Arabia).

The primary U.S. concerns in the early days of the Iraqi invasion of Kuwait were oil and the fate of Saudi Arabia. In a nationally televised address on August 8, 1990, the president announced that the United States would use military force to repel the invasion, and the main motivation he gave for the use of military force was America's energy needs. He said, "Our country now imports nearly half the oil it consumes and could face a major threat to its economic independence. . . . The sovereign independence of Saudi Arabia is of vital interest to the United States."

Appearing before the Senate Armed Services Committee on September 11, 1990, Secretary of Defense Cheney said, "Once [Saddam] acquired Kuwait and deployed an army as large as the one he possesses, he would be in a position to be able to dictate the future of world-wide energy policy, and that [would give] him a stranglehold on our economy."

While other justifications for the war, such as liberating Kuwait, were given, experts agree that the Gulf War in 1990–1991 was the first war in world history almost entirely about oil. But while the Gulf War was the first war over oil, it won't be the last.

Unless there are drastic changes in U.S. consumption, by 2030 the United States will import twice as much oil as it did in 1996, and since most of that oil comes from the Middle East, U.S. actions to protect these interests will increase as well. Most of Europe and Japan are more dependent on imports than the United States. They too must protect their future supply of energy from the Middle East to protect their economic interests. The Middle East/Persian Gulf will continue to be the focus of the world.

THE INVASION OF IRAQ

Why was the world surprised when the United States invaded Iraq in 2003? No matter what the excuse, it is evident that the nation is willing to pay almost any price to control events in the Middle East. History books will have to settle the issue of whether the war began because of hard evidence that Saddam was building weapons of mass destruction or simply to establish military control of the region and the flow of oil to the West.

In fact, the entire region is now less stable than it was before the invasion. The American-led war in Iraq has cost more than $200 billion and continues to inflict a high cost in human lives because of thousands of military and civilian casualties. Radical Islamic terrorism has been given a new justification to hate the great Satan of the West and a convenient place to begin the battle. Iran has been emboldened by the U.S. distraction in Iraq and is flexing its muscles in a dramatic bid for regional supremacy. Iran is also seizing the opportunity to fuel terror in Iraq—stoking the Sunni–Shiite division.

The fiction that one superpower like America can occupy a country, restore order, and secure the export of oil to the West is now gone. In short, occupying forces cannot protect the wellheads and pipelines from sabotage. And they cannot stop the kidnapping and killing of civilian workers. In *The End of Oil*, Paul Roberts notes:

> *In fact, the greatest casualty of the Iraq war may be the very idea of energy security.*
>
> *But with the continuing fiasco in Iraq, it is now clear that even the most powerful military entity in world history cannot stabilize a country at will or "make it" produce oil simply by sending in soldiers and tanks. In other words, since the Iraq invasion, the oil market now understands that the United States cannot guarantee the security of oil supplies . . . for itself or for anyone else. That new and chilling knowledge, as much as anything else, explains the high price of oil.[18]*

Whether out of fear of weapons of mass destruction or simply concern that the region will ignite and tensions in the region will spin out of control, the United States once again has attempted to control events in the Middle East with American troops.

THE TERRIBLE DILEMMA FACING THE UNITED STATES

The United States finds itself in a very difficult position as the only superpower in the world. Its economic and military power is dependent on oil from the Middle East and OPEC nations, so it has made several pledges related to this region:

1. The United States has promised to protect the State of Israel and has supplied Israel with the most sophisticated weapons and equipment available.

2. The United States has proven it will protect its vital interests in the Middle East by "any means necessary, including military force."
3. The United States has pledged to attack any nation that openly supports terrorism and did so in Afghanistan.
4. The United States has pledged to control weapons of mass destruction anywhere they are a threat to Israel or the United States.

This situation will only get more difficult, and the cost to protect America's interests in the Middle East will increase dramatically. Europe is also a major stakeholder in this crisis. In a severe crisis it does not appear that the United States alone can solve this problem. The West must create new alliances to protect its interests. Unstable prices or the loss of the oil supply could destroy the economic fiber of the West. The Middle East and the Persian Gulf will continue to be the focus of world attention, and any major crisis that engulfs the region will bring an international cry for peace.

END-TIME PROPHECY IN THE MAKING

The Bible predicts that a new alignment of nations will emerge to control events in the Middle East (see Daniel 9:27; 11:40-45). A coalition of ten world leaders will consolidate the power of the West into an iron fist. Until very recently there has not been a threat to the Western world that could cause such a shift in the balance of power. But Europe's industrialized nations must have a secure, guaranteed flow of oil and security from the social disruption of Islamic terror imported from the Middle East. The political and economic implications to the world would be no less than those occurring when the Roman Empire combined many nations into one political and economic unity to dominate the world and enforce the *Pax Romana* (Roman Peace).

The Middle East is about to explode and drag the world into one of the most difficult and terrifying conflicts in world history. The time between the cycles of violence in the Middle East crisis is shortening. The bloodshed over oil and power has just begun. Deep-seated passions, religious fanaticism, and poverty fuel suicidal terrorism. Countries in the region will not be able to resolve this crisis on their own.

Terrorism, instability, and the threat of a disruption in oil have created a greater need for peace than any international situation since the Cold War. Outside nations must protect their interests and stop the bloodshed. The prophets of the Old Testament predicted just such a situation. From a biblical standpoint this is the most dramatic evidence that the world is now headed down the road to Armageddon.

The Prophetic Destiny of the Middle East

Civilization began in the Middle East with the creation of Adam and Eve. It was there that the great empires of the past rose and fell—Egypt, Assyria, Babylon, Medo-Persia, Greece, and Rome.

It will be in the Middle East that the future world government will have its center of political and economic power. The enigma of how the underdeveloped Middle East could once again become the center of world history has suddenly been solved by the world's economic dependence on oil and the worldwide need to stop Islamic terrorism. Already strategic geographically as the hub of three continents, the Middle East is destined to be the center of a world struggle for wealth and power so great that it will engulf the entire world in a gigantic battle centered in the valley of Meggido—also known as Armageddon.

The Coming Crisis—How Far Away?

The coming crisis in the Middle East is looming. Western civilization would be brought to its knees by a sudden disruption in the supply of oil. Whether by terror, nuclear exchange, or a bidding war for oil—it could happen suddenly and without warning. The world's need for carbon-based fuel is rapidly approaching the breaking point. The Middle

East is the only place where that thirst can be quenched. Alternative fuel for transportation worldwide is ten to twenty years away. If the Middle East is to rise to power, now is its hour of opportunity. If Islamic terrorism is to attain its goals, it must act soon.

See how today's headlines relate to this chapter at
http://www.prophecyhotline.com.

CHAPTER 3

TERRORISM REACHES EVERYONE

EVENT #2: Islamic terrorism fueled by hatred of the West and Israel pushes the world to the brink of total chaos.

To achieve such sweeping change, bin Laden espouses
a strategy that turns on one premise: The believers
must attack World Infidelity, in the form of the United
States and its allies, head-on. . . . The concomitant
requirement for such a strategy is that violence against
the United States has to be catastrophic. . . . The killing
must be on a grand scale.

DANIEL BENJAMIN AND STEVEN SIMON, *THE NEXT ATTACK*

The world today is a more dangerous place
than at any time in history.

BILL O'REILLY, *THE O'REILLY FACTOR*

THE EVENTS OF 9/11 STRUCK to the very core of the American way
of life and national psyche. For the first time in their history, Americans no longer felt safe and invulnerable to attack on U.S. soil.

In the wake of the tragedy, we have all become familiar with
the Homeland Security Advisory System. The color-coded graphic

contains five levels that grade the perceived risk of terrorist attack. The five levels are: low, guarded, elevated, high, and severe. The threat of a terrorist attack is a new aspect of everyday life in America. But even now we hardly notice. For most people it really does not seem to matter much whether the threat is low or high.

Suicide attacks, insurrections, and riots have kept world attention on this gathering threat. Terror dominates the headlines. But violence always seems to erupt somewhere else. The wishful thinking is that the trouble will always be "over there."

Israel is definitely in the center of the terror bull's-eye. From the beginning of the Al-Aqsa Intifada (uprising) in September 2000, over one thousand Israelis (mostly civilians) have been killed by terrorists. More than four thousand Palestinians have died as well. And the attacks

A Brief History of the Worldwide Islamic Terror Network

Al-Qaeda means "the base" in Arabic. It was founded in Afghanistan in 1979 by Osama bin Laden. When most people think of Al-Qaeda they only think of 9/11; however, there have been about a dozen major Al-Qaeda attacks worldwide since 9/11.

Hamas is an acronym of the Arabic *Harakat al-Muqawama al-Islamiya*, which means "Islamic Resistance Movement." The word *Hamas* corresponds to an Arabic word meaning "enthusiasm." Hamas was founded in the Gaza Strip in 1987 for the express purpose of eliminating Israel. It is funded by Iran, Palestinian expatriates, and private benefactors in other Arab states. Hamas is responsible for over one hundred homicide bombings in Israel. In January 2006, Hamas won a surprise victory over the Fatah Party in the Palestinian parliamentary elections, taking 76 of the 132 seats.

Hezbollah, which means "Party of God," was founded in 1982 by followers of Iranian cleric Ayatollah Khomeini as an arm of Iran with the chief purpose of destroying Israel and as a means to create an Islamic republic in Lebanon. It is funded and armed by Iran through Syria. Estimates of Iranian support for Hezbollah range from $100 to $300 million per year. Hezbollah has funded and aided Al-Qaeda. Hezbollah was responsible for the bombing of the U.S. Embassy in Beirut in 1983 that killed 63 people and the truck bomb that destroyed the U.S. Marine barracks in Lebanon in 1983 that killed 241 U.S. soldiers.

continue. Hamas, an avowed terrorist organization that refuses even to recognize Israel's right to exist, is now in control of the Palestinian Authority. Hezbollah has gained stature in the Muslim world after squaring off with Israel for thirty-four days in the summer of 2006. It is now firmly embedded to Israel's north in Lebanon.

Increasingly, the United States is being attacked for its support of Israel. This has much more far-reaching implications for our lives than we have imagined. Islamic terror and its threat to the peace and security of the West could be a key signpost on the road to the end times.

TERROR COMES TO AMERICA

Terrorism, fueled by fanatical Islamic ideology, has reared its ugly head over and over again in the last twenty-five years. For the United States it began with the Iranian hostage crisis in 1979. The next attack occurred when Hezbollah bombed the U.S. Embassy in Beirut in 1983, killing 63 people. Then on October 23, 1983—also in Beirut—a truck bomb slammed into a U.S. Marine barracks, killing 241 U.S. soldiers.

Islamic terror first came to American soil on February 26, 1993, when a truck bomb was exploded in the World Trade Center in New York City. This was a dreadful portent of the rising threat to America and the world. But few realized the ominous nature of that event at that time.

On September 11, 2001, the entire world was awakened suddenly to the awfulness of the new global threat—a threat unlike anything the world has ever seen. Feeding on hate for the West and Israel, a well-organized network of Islamic radicals had begun its open warfare with the United States. This was the first stunning attack that gripped the nation, but it was only the portent of many more.

TERROR IS EVERYWHERE

Islamic terrorists hit Bali, Indonesia, on October 12, 2002, killing 202.

On the eve of national elections, four trains in Madrid, Spain, were

39

hit on March 11, 2004. The attacks altered elections in Spain and led to the country's withdrawal from the war in Iraq.

Terror struck Great Britain on July 7, 2005, when four bombs in central London were detonated in a span of fifty-six minutes, killing 37 and injuring 700. It was the worst attack in London since the blitz of World War II.

For at least eleven consecutive nights in late 2005, France endured riots that spread to 300 French cities. The rioters, who mainly targeted vehicles, were primarily youths born of Arab and African immigrants in poor suburbs. About 5,000 cars were torched—1,400 on one night (November 6) alone. France's far-right political party, the National Front, emerged stronger than ever after the civil unrest.

Muslim fury erupted all over the world as angry rioters demonstrated for days in February 2006 over a cartoon in a Danish newspaper that depicted the prophet Mohammad as a terrorist. Iran and Syria did all they could to fan the flames. Riots broke out in places such as Pakistan, India, Indonesia, Norway, and Thailand. This proved that any incident can provoke protests, riots, and terrorist attacks around the world, thanks to instant worldwide news and the Internet.

It's clear that Islamic extremism and terror have gone global. Part of the frustration with terror is that it lurks in the shadows. It relies on stealth to commit its dastardly deeds. It uses the Internet to spread the ideology and tactics of terrorism to every corner of the world. Nameless, faceless terrorists patiently and painstakingly weave their web of destruction in secret. With an enemy like this, conventional military strength is often of little use. The world faces a totally unconventional enemy that aims to push Western civilization back into the Dark Ages.

While many members of Al-Qaeda and other terrorist cells have been captured or killed, for the most part terrorists are hard to find and sometimes almost impossible to root out. Osama bin Laden orchestrated the 9/11 attacks in September 2001 and disappeared into hiding while continuing to release murderous messages of encouragement to his followers. For every terrorist that is killed or captured, several more are easily recruited from refugee camps, mosques, or the disen-franchised Muslim minority across Europe.

WMDS AND TERROR

How serious is the threat of worldwide terror? Could it really spread to everyone? Could the whole world feel its fury?

It took only three years for the United States to build the world's first atom bomb. The Soviets went nuclear in the 1940s, the Chinese in the late 1960s, India in the 1970s, and Pakistan in the 1990s. All of these countries set off nuclear tests to prove they had achieved their objec-tive. Even before North Korea conducted a nuclear test in 2006, it was widely assumed that it had created as many as ten nuclear weapons.

And where is Iran on the road to achieving its nuclear objectives? It took Pakistan and North Korea roughly a decade to get enough mate-rial for their first nuclear devices. Iran has been pushing to go nuclear for two decades. For more than a decade it has played a game of nuclear hide-and-seek with the International Atomic Energy Agency.

Intelligence sources have long believed that Abdul Qadeer Khan, who is credited with developing Pakistan's nuclear bomb, sold both the design and actual P-2 centrifuges needed to create enriched uranium to Libya, North Korea, and Iran. Khan sold Libya a complete Chinese-made bomb design and most likely sold the same design to Iran.[1] It is difficult to deter-mine who is now in possession of this type of sensitive information.

Still the world was startled when Iran's president, Mahmoud Ahmadinejad, announced in April 2006 that Iran was already conduct-ing research on the P-2 centrifuge that would quadruple its ability to enrich uranium. In August 2006 intelligence sources predicted that Iran would have hundreds of P-2 centrifuges by 2007.[2] Centrifuges of advanced design are necessary to produce concentrations of uranium's rare component, uranium 235. Although Ahmadinejad's claim may have been an exaggeration, it certainly raised serious concerns.

Uranium must be enriched to levels close to 90 percent for use in atomic bombs. The world is not sure how or when Iran will assemble its first atomic bomb. Estimates vary, but most informed sources believe that Iran will build its first atomic bomb sometime within the next three to five years unless the program is disrupted by an attack from outside Iran. And, of course, Iran could speed this timetable dramatically by purchasing an atomic weapon from North Korea.[3]

Beginning in 2004, the Senate Foreign Relations Committee, chaired by Indiana senator Richard Lugar, surveyed analysts around the world to assess the potential threat from weapons of mass destruction. After the study was complete, Senator Lugar released this statement: "The bottom line is this: For the foreseeable future, the United States and other nations will face an existential threat from the intersection of terrorism and weapons of mass destruction."[4]

After polling eighty-five nonproliferation and national security experts, the authors of this report estimated the risk of attack by weapons of mass destruction to be as high as 70 percent by the year 2015. Most of the experts said they expect one or two new countries to acquire nuclear weapons by 2010 and as many as five by 2015.

The report from the survey also contained these findings:

- The most significant risk of a WMD attack was from a radiological weapon, the so-called "dirty bomb," in which radioactive material is put into a conventional explosive device.
- The threat that a dirty bomb will be detonated and affect a major portion of a city by 2015 was judged to be 40 percent.
- The next highest risk was an attack with a chemical or biological weapon.
- The risk of attack with conventional nuclear weapons was judged to be 16.4 percent by 2010 and 29.2 percent by 2015.[5]

TERROR AND THE TIME OF THE END

The combination of radical Islam and terror is the great new threat to the world. But what are the prophetic implications of this new menace?

The rise of Islamic terror seems to be setting the stage for the end times in at least four important ways. Let's consider each of them briefly:

1. **Time is running out.** The predictions in the Senate Foreign Relations Committee report are sobering and ominous, especially in a post 9/11 world where Iran's nuclear threat adds to the already gathering storm. A dark shadow hangs over our world. It seems like the coming of Christ could be very near. Why? Stop and think about it. End-time events predicted by the prophets of the Bible have never been so easy to imagine or so consistent with the movement of world history.

   The Bible predicts that God—not man—will bring the period of the Gentiles to an abrupt halt during the Battle of Armageddon when Christ returns to judge the world. God, not man, will control the events that lead to the reign of Christ on earth, when the Jewish people will finally be ushered into their hour of glory and peace predicted by the prophets. The lion will lie down with the lamb. The earth will be saved for the predicted millennial reign of Christ. According to the Scriptures, at the end of that reign, God, not man, will dismantle the earth and create a new heaven and new earth.

   If rogue nations or terrorists begin to use WMDs, the whole world will be thrown into chaos and confusion. Just think what would happen if one of these weapons, even a dirty bomb, was detonated in a major city in the United States or Europe. While something this catastrophic could happen to destabilize the world before the Rapture of the church, it seems much more likely that these kinds of international convulsions will be part of the post-Rapture scenario that catapults the Group of Ten and eventually the Antichrist to world power.

   Of course, God could delay or turn back the timetable for these end-time events. He could prevent terrorists or rogue nations from getting their hands on WMDs and pushing the world to the brink of chaos. But right now it looks like the stage is set for end-time events to begin, though no one on earth knows the day or the hour of Christ's coming.

2. **The nations are in place for the predicted invasion of Israel.** The rise of Islamic terror is setting the stage for the events in Ezekiel 38–39. These chapters prophesy an invasion of Israel in the end times by a vast coalition of nations, all of whom are Islamic today except Russia. Israel has said that a new "axis of terror"—Iran, Syria, and the Hamas-run Palestinian government—is sowing the seeds of the first world war of the twenty-first century. The rise of Islam, and especially radical Islamic terrorism, strikingly foreshadows Ezekiel's great prophecy. More details about this incredible prophecy will be presented in detail in chapter 7.

3. **The conditions are in place for the world to accept peace at any price.** The world is more at risk today for nuclear detonations, biological warfare, and chemical warfare than ever before. Pakistan and India have the bomb. So do China and North Korea. Iran is working feverishly to join the "nuclear club." It's only a matter of time until rogue states, terrorists, or fanatics get their hands on these weapons of mass destruction. The unrest in key Islamic nations could easily erupt into an explosive call for widespread jihad, or holy war.

Moreover, the Middle East is the only region in the world whose reserves are large enough to meet rising U.S. and international demands for oil. This deadly combination of oil and terror in the Middle East leaves the West especially vulnerable.

In this climate of terror and uncertainty, the world yearns for some way to make the unrest stop. People the world over are clamoring for peace. People are also yearning for safety. The world has become obsessed with security. We have never felt more unsafe, more exposed, more vulnerable, than we do right now. We want safety: safety for ourselves, safety for our children, safety from a nuclear nightmare, safety from terrorist bombings, safety from bioterrorism, safety from chemical warfare. People will naturally begin to search for someone who can make sense out of it all—someone, anyone, who can bring peace when the world is on the brink of disaster.

Of course, this longing is nothing new. But with the rise of fanatics and war by stealth—the sudden, unexpected strike of terrorism—the cry for peace and safety has become a worldwide cadence. As terror and disruption of the supply of oil collide, the world will be willing to pay any price for peace in the Middle East. This is just the scenario that will catapult a leader to the world stage to consolidate power and promise peace to a world on the brink of disaster.

4. **Globalism would allow one man to declare himself world ruler.** The scourge of global terror has served to bring the world together. After the flood of the earth recorded in Genesis, the Bible says that all the people of the world congregated at one location under the leadership of one man, Nimrod, to build a great tower to the heavens (Genesis 10:8-10; 11:1-9). The whole world was one community in global rebellion against its Creator. God came down and confounded the language of man, dispersing the rebel race over the face of the earth.

Ever since that time, Satan has tried in vain to again bring the world under the control of one man through whom he could rule the world. The pharaohs, Nebuchadnezzar, Alexander the Great, the caesars, Napoleon, Hitler, and Stalin have entered and left the stage of world history.

The Bible predicts that in the end times the world will once again come together in a one-world economy, government, and religion to shake its collective fist in the face of the Creator. The Antichrist will lead this global union against God (Revelation 13:3-18).

Until recently it would have been impossible for one world ruler to instantaneously communicate with the entire world and control the world economy. But all that has changed dramatically. The 1990s have been called the decade of globalization. Incredible developments occurred that advanced globalization at warp speed. Here are just a few of the main contributors.

- The end of the Cold War
- The creation of the World Trade Organization
- The advance of the Internet
- The creation of CNN and instant global news
- The need for global cooperation on environmental issues
- The threat of terror worldwide
- The global need for oil

The world that seemed so large, expansive, and hopelessly fragmented only a few decades ago now seems small and interconnected.

In the face of the terror threat, nations can no longer afford to go it alone. Those in the West, especially, must rely on one another. Isolation is a thing of the past. International cooperation is necessary to share critical intelligence and surveillance information to stop the advance of terrorism.

Worldwide terror is bringing the world together. The Antichrist will take advantage of this opportunity created by fear and will seize control of the global network of nations to rule the world.

TRUE PEACE IS COMING

God will allow even that which is evil to advance His prophetic program. The false peace offered by the Antichrist will be shattered, followed by the catastrophic judgments that end the period of the Gentiles. God, not man, will bring true peace to earth. It's hard to imagine world peace in these troubled times. But it is coming. There will be real, permanent, universal peace when, and only when, the Prince of Peace comes to rule over the earth.

 See how today's headlines relate to this chapter at *http://www.prophecyhotline.com.*

CHAPTER 4

ISRAEL: GROUND ZERO FOR THE END TIMES

EVENT #3: Israel aggressively defends itself in a sea of enemies—bringing the world to the brink of World War III.

> The Jewish people have unchallengeable, eternal, historic right to the Land of Israel, the inheritance of their forefathers.
>
> FORMER ISRAELI PRIME MINISTER MENACHEM BEGIN

> Israel is exceptionally strong and knows how to defend itself.
>
> FORMER ISRAELI PRIME MINISTER SHIMON PERES

ON ANCIENT MAPS ISRAEL WAS often placed at the center, signifying that it was at the center of man's activity. While Israel is no longer in the middle of the world map, it still occupies the center place in world headlines. Stop and think about it. It's very difficult to pick up a newspaper or news magazine, or watch a cable news program, and not read or hear something about Israel. Notice this the next time you read the paper or listen to the world headlines on the evening news. Israel is everywhere. There's the Israeli-Palestinian quagmire, terrorist attacks, peace talks, land for peace, the Gaza pullout, the war with Hezbollah and Hamas, and critical elections. And this is nothing new. It's been this way for at least thirty years.

Israel is the nation at the center—the center of politics, terrorism, the peace talks, and jihadist hatred.

Have you ever wondered why? Why is Israel so important? Why all the fuss over a Middle Eastern nation that's no bigger than New Jersey? The reason goes all the way back to Abraham and reaches forward to the end of time.

Israel. It's the key. History proclaims its past. Headlines proclaim its present. Prophecy proclaims its future.[1]

THE HORIZONTAL VIEW OF PROPHECY

The promises and prophecies pertaining to Israel are intricately interwoven throughout the entire Bible. Some involve general promises, but most involve specific and detailed glimpses into the future. When the prophets described future events, it was as if they were looking horizontally at distant mountain peaks. They described these peaks of history in vivid detail but often had little understanding of the vast valleys of time that separated the events they described.[2]

The "Mountain Peaks" of Prophecy

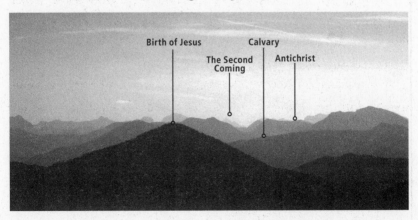

Many of the prophecies about Israel are especially confusing unless they are carefully fitted together and compared to the history of the Jewish people and the Land of Promise. Jerusalem has been destroyed many times. Three times the Jews have been scattered from the land—and three times they have returned. The prophecies of their scattering and return must be compared to the actual historical facts. It is important to ask what prophecies have been fulfilled and which can be expected to be fulfilled in the future. Many ancient prophecies that have not yet taken place may well occur within our lifetime. The prophecies in the Bible make it clear that Israel's past, present, and future are key to what will happen next in the world.

Prophetic Questions about the Promised Land

When the biblical promises and prophecies speak of the Promised Land, do they describe an actual land with geographic boundaries? Is this literal or figurative language? If the promise of the land pertains to an actual geographic location, have the Jews ever possessed it? Does the land really belong to them?

If the land was promised and prophesied as a reward for obedience, is it possible that disobedience and unbelief have caused the promise to be withdrawn? Is the promise restated in the New Testament? Are there conditions to that promise?

The answer to these important questions requires a further investigation into the specifics of the promises and prophecies about Israel. These specifics must then be compared to the actual history of the Jewish people and the Land of Promise.

To really understand the present and its deep-seated issues and struggles in the Middle East, we have to go all the way back to the days of Abraham and the promises God made to him. To see into the future we have to look back to the past.

Abram, the Man of Destiny

In the twentieth century, the world witnessed one of the greatest miracles of history—the restoration of an ancient people to the land of their fathers after centuries of being scattered among every nation of the world. The story of Israel's return, stirring as it is, has deep roots that reach back four thousand years to the city of Ur of the Chaldees, an ancient city in Mesopotamia located not far from Babylon. It was there that Abram, a man of destiny, lived in a city of advanced culture. To Abram came the command to leave the land of his fathers and go to a land God would show him.

The story of Abram begins in Genesis 11:27 and ends with his death in Genesis 25:8. In a book that devotes only three chapters to describing the origin of the world, fourteen chapters are devoted to the life of Abram.

In partial obedience to God's command to go to a new land, Abram left his home and became a tent dweller, moving about seven hundred miles to the northwest to Haran, where he lived until his father died. Then another pilgrimage, this time about five hundred miles to the southwest, brought him to the Land of Promise. It was there that Abram lived and died.

To Abram, a man of destiny, God gave great promises. He promised Abram would become the father of a great nation, that he would become famous and be a blessing to others (Genesis 12:2). Additionally, God promised that all the families of the earth would be blessed through Abram. History has recorded the literal fulfillment of these promises. The name Abram, later changed to Abraham, meaning "father of nations," has been a great name, revered alike by Jew, Christian, and Muslim. Not only the Jewish people but the whole Arab world descended from Abraham.

As promised, God has given Abraham so many descendants that, like dust or the stars in the night sky, they could not be counted (Genesis 13:16; 15:5). Through Abraham came the prophets, the writers of the Scriptures of the Old and New Testaments, and Jesus Christ—the Son of Abraham, the Son of David. Those who have blessed the descendants of Abraham have been blessed; those who have cursed the sons of Abraham have been cursed (Genesis 12:3). The judgments of God have fallen upon Israel's oppressors—Egypt, Assyria, Babylon, Rome, and in more modern times, Spain, Germany, and Russia. The final judgments will come when the period of the Gentiles ends.

The Promise of the Land

In the center of God's promises to Abraham was the promise to give his descendants a land. The whole drama of Abraham's life revolved around his willingness to leave Ur of the Chaldees to go to a new Land of Promise. The promise did not simply involve spiritual blessing; the lifelong pilgrimage of Abraham was a necessary part of the fulfillment of the promise for a land.

In Genesis 15 the confirmation of the promise is stated in no uncertain terms. Abraham's faith in leaving his home to receive this land was rewarded with a detailed explanation of the promise. The biblical narrative presents the description of the land in definite terms with clear geographic boundaries, and it even indicates the peoples who inhabited the land at that time: "So the LORD made a covenant with Abram that day and said, 'I have given this land to your descendants, all the way from the border of Egypt to the great Euphrates River—the land now occupied by the Kenites, Kenizzites, Kadmonites, Hittites, Perizzites, Rephaites, Amorites, Canaanites, Girgashites, and Jebusites'" (Genesis 15:18-21).

This biblical account clearly referred to a specific geographical land, not some general blessing or a promise of heaven. The continued revelation of God to Abram elaborated the promise again as recorded in Genesis 17. Here Abram's name was changed to Abraham because of the promise that he would be the father of many nations.

The promise of the land is tied to the promise of a continuing heritage: "I will confirm my covenant with you and your descendants after you, from generation to generation. This is the everlasting covenant: I will always be your God and the God of your descendants after you. And I will give the entire land of Canaan, where you now live as a foreigner, to you and your descendants. It will be their possession forever, and I will be their God" (Genesis 17:7-8).

The meaning to Abraham and the early readers of Scripture is evident. The land promised was Israel, stretching from the Sinai Desert north and east to the Euphrates River. This would include all the holdings of present-day Israel, Lebanon, and the West Bank of Jordan, plus substantial portions of Syria, Iraq, and Saudi Arabia. And remarkably, as described in Genesis 17, the covenant was described as an everlasting covenant, and the land of Canaan promised as an everlasting possession.

In light of the raging controversy over who owns the land of Israel, it's important to remember that the only specific piece of land on this earth that God ever promised to any people was the land of Israel, described in Genesis 15, to the Jewish people.

While God promised the land to Abraham, he never possessed it. He was one hundred years old when God miraculously enabled him to have a son, Isaac, to fulfill His promises. But even after the birth of Isaac, Abraham did not possess the land, except for the small portion that he bought as a burial plot for Sarah. Instead, God plainly told him that his descendants for hundreds of years would not possess the land. They would, in fact, be strangers in a foreign land, where they would be oppressed as slaves. After four generations they could return to the land when the sin of the Amorites had run its course (Genesis 15:13-16).

History records that the Jewish people have been exiled from their land on three major occasions in the past and that they have been supernaturally restored to their land by God each time. The chart below gives a very concise overview of Israel's past departures and providential returns.

The Israelites' Departures and Returns

DEPARTURES	RETURNS
First Departure: Egypt	**First Return:** Under Moses
Second Departure: 10 northern tribes by Assyria in 722 BC; 2 southern tribes by Babylon in 605–586 BC.	**Second Return:** Under Zerubbabel (538 BC), Ezra (458 BC), and Nehemiah (444 BC)
Third Departure: Romans in AD 70	**Third Return:** Began in 1871 and continues today

Prophetic Hope for a Last Return

With each of the first two departures, there was a glorious return. But what about the third departure? Jesus clearly predicted that the magnificent Temple of His lifetime would be completely demolished so that not one stone would be left on top of another (Matthew 24:2). The fate of Jerusalem and the Jewish people was understood to take a drastic turn for the worse within the lifetime of the generation that heard His message. And, of course, the prophecy of Jesus was literally fulfilled in AD 70 when the Roman army under the emperor Titus destroyed Jerusalem and the Temple. But the nagging questions remained: Was Israel finished? Were the promises to be set aside?

The apostle Paul, himself an Israelite, struggled with these very questions. His conclusion was simply an emphatic *no*! "I ask, then, has God rejected his own people, the nation of Israel? Of course not!" (Romans 11:1).

Would there be a fulfillment of the everlasting covenant to possess the land, a land with clear geographic boundaries promised as an everlasting possession? The writer of the book of Hebrews reviewed the promises to Abraham. Were they conditioned on Israel's obedience, thereby nullified because of Israel's disbelief? No, they were not. The final outcome was immutable, unchangeable. For example, there was God's promise to Abraham.

Since there was no one greater to swear by, God took an oath in his own name. . . . God also bound himself with an oath, so that those who received the promise could be perfectly sure that he would never change his mind. So God has given both his promise and his oath. These two things are unchangeable because it is impossible for God to lie. Therefore, we who have fled to him for refuge can have great confidence as we hold to the hope that lies before us. This hope is a strong and trustworthy anchor for our souls. It leads us through the curtain into God's inner sanctuary. (Hebrews 6:13, 17-19)

The succinct and straightforward testimony of both the Old and New Testaments points to a final return to the land promised. This hope of restoration has sustained the Jews through nineteen hundred years of struggle. Christians who have understood the clear prophetic witness of the Bible have expected it to happen for hundreds of years, even when the odds were overwhelmingly against it. Some of the key events leading to this prophecy's fulfillment are described below.

Scattered persecutions. The centuries that followed AD 70 were tragic for Jews. Afflicted by persecutions of incredible severity, their total number at one time shrank to approximately one million. Hated by professing Christians and non-Christians alike, they were driven from land to land, never finding rest or prosperity except for brief periods of time.

From all outward appearances, Israel's future was hopeless. In the seventh century the Arabs took possession of Israel's ancient land. In the twelfth century the Christian crusaders were established in Israel for a brief time but were finally defeated by Saladin in 1187. The Ottoman Turks took over in 1517 and continued their control over the Promised Land until Turkey was defeated in World War I. A dramatic turn of events began in 1917 when General Allenby conquered Jerusalem, and the British occupation of Palestine (Israel) began.

Beginnings of the third return. The return of Jews to the land was beset by many problems, although as early as 1871 a few Jews had managed to return to the land, and about twenty-five thousand Jews had settled there by 1881. The idea of the Jews repossessing their ancient land was not stated in any formal way, however, until it was adopted in the first Zionist congress, called in 1897 by Theodor Herzl. The goal of reclaiming the land of Palestine as a home for the wandering Jews, although seemingly an idealistic dream, brought the light of hope to Jewish eyes around the world.

The Balfour Declaration of 1917. The progress was painfully slow. By 1914 the number of Jews in the land had reached only eighty thousand. During World War I, to gain support of Jews for the war effort, the British foreign secretary, Arthur J. Balfour, issued the Balfour Declaration on November 2, 1917. This declaration indicated approval of Israel's goal: "His Majesty's Government views with favor the establishment in Palestine of a national home for the Jewish people." Pressure from the Arab world, which would have no part in establishing a home for Israel, and the desire of Britain to maintain friendship with the Arab nations, prevented any fulfillment of this promise. Little progress had been made when World War II broke out in 1939. By that time, however, four hundred thousand Jews had managed to find their way into the country in spite of severe restrictions on Jewish immigration and laws that did not allow Jews to possess real estate.

The state of Israel established in 1948. Many anti-Semitic historical revisionists, such as Iran's president, Mahmoud Ahmadinejad, deny that the Jewish Holocaust ever occurred. However, World War II, which resulted in the terrible massacre of millions of Jews under Nazi tyranny, created a favorable attitude and worldwide sympathy for the Jewish people. Certainly there should be some place where the wandering Jew could have a home. Although an Arab League was formed in 1945 to oppose Jewish expansion, the United Nations created a home for Jews in Palestine after World War II with the approval of the United States and Russia. The directive stated that Palestine should be divided into a Jewish state and an Arab state, and five thousand square miles were assigned to the infant state of Israel.

Israeli-Arab War, 1948–1949. On May 14, 1948, when British control ended, Israel became an independent state for the first time in hundreds of years. The population of the new nation included six hundred and fifty thousand Jews and many hundreds of thousands of Arabs. The settlement, however, was quite unacceptable to the Arab world. Israel was attacked on all sides by Egypt, Jordan, Iraq, Syria, Lebanon, and Saudi Arabia. Israel's defense was heroic, and the armies of her opponents were disorganized. Although thousands of Israelis fell in battle, by the time a truce was arranged on January 7, 1949, Israel had extended her area of possession from five thousand square miles to eight thousand square miles, including much of the Negev, the great desert to the south. Israel's history from that date to this has been one of unending trouble, recurring warfare, ongoing attempts at peace, but gradual strengthening of the nation.

Israel's Time Line from 1948

1948	The state of Israel declares its independence and is attacked by five Arab nations.
1949	Jerusalem is divided into two parts (New City under Jewish rule; Old City under Jordanian rule).
1956	Israel, Great Britain, and France capture the Sinai from Egypt.
1964	The PLO is established.
1967	In the Six-Day War (June 6–11), Israel defeats Egypt, Syria, and Jordan and gains control of all Jerusalem, the Golan Heights, the West Bank of the Jordan River and the Gaza Strip.
1973	On Yom Kippur (Day of Atonement) Egypt and Syria launch a surprise attack against Israel, but Israel turns them back.
1979	Israel and Egypt sign the Camp David Accords, in which Israel agrees to return the Sinai Peninsula to Egypt in exchange for peace.
1982	Israel invades Lebanon in what was known as Operation Peace of Galilee.
1987–1993	The first Intifada (Palestinian uprising) erupts in the West Bank and Gaza Strip.
1991	During the first Gulf War, Israel is hit by Iraqi Scud missiles.
1993	The Oslo Accords are signed. Israeli prime minister Yitzhak Rabin and PLO chairman Yasser Arafat shake hands at the White House.
2000	Israel withdraws from Lebanon. The second Intifada erupts in September when Ariel Sharon visits the Temple Mount.
2003	The United States presents the "Road Map" for peace in the Middle East.
2005	Israel pulls out of all twenty-one settlements in the Gaza Strip.
2006	Israel wages a bloody 34-day war against Hezbollah for the return of kidnapped soldiers (while also trying to secure the release of a soldier abducted by Hamas just a few weeks before Hezbollah's provocation).

HAVE THE PROPHECIES BEEN FULFILLED?

From the time of the promise to Abraham to the present hour, the prophecies about Israel's total possession and blessing in the land have not yet been fulfilled. The pulse of Jewish history, with three successive departures from and three returns to their Promised Land, has been a dramatic one. The most dramatic events, however, are still ahead. Is the present return of Israel the beginning of the last and ultimate regathering of Israel? Is this one more in a series of current events preparing the way for the end of the period of the Gentiles? As non-Jewish nations jockey into position for their last moments of glory and judgment, the stage is set for the final end-time events predicted as the end of the period of the Gentiles. Then and only then will Israel finally experience all that has been promised and hoped for since the time of Abraham.

The year 2006 appears to have been a key turning point in the regathering of the Jewish people to their homeland. In 2006, for the first time in about 1,900 years, Israel became home to the largest Jewish community in the world, surpassing even the Jewish population in the United States. From a population of about 650,000 when the Jewish state was founded in 1948, the Jewish population of Israel grew to more than 5.3 million in 2006. It is expected to grow to more than 6 million by 2020. The restoration of the Jewish state and return of all twelve tribes to Israel are necessary preconditions for the events of the end times to be fulfilled.

But the return of the Jews to Israel has been no easy road to glory. Negotiations for peace in the Middle East have not produced a lasting peace. The doves and peacemakers in Israel will eventually lead their country into a peace that will compromise their security in the hope of economic prosperity. It is sad to forecast that a nation that defended herself so bravely for fifty years will be lulled into a false peace with international guarantees that will be of no help in the final hour the Bible describes as "such a time of terror. It will be a time of trouble for my people Israel" (Jeremiah 30:7).

The outline of prophecy is self-evident. After their initial return, the Jews will go through a period of false peace, an international betrayal, and a bloodbath of astounding proportions. Without the direct intervention of God, both Israel and the Jewish people would be completely destroyed.

The Old Testament prophet Jeremiah describes the time of trouble for Israel in vivid terms. This is the last three and a half years of the seven-year tribulation period leading to the final battle—the Battle of Armageddon. It will begin when the false peace with Israel is broken by the new leader of the Group of Ten.

This period of history is often called "the great tribulation" and a time of "greater anguish than at any time since world began" (Revelation 7:14; Matthew 24:21). It is detailed in the book of Revelation as a specific time ending the period of the Gentiles. Israel, Jerusalem, and the Temple rebuilt during the peace will be "turned over to the nations. They will trample the holy city for 42 months" (Revelation 11:2).

After promising the Israelites' return, Jeremiah warned, "This is what the LORD says: 'I hear cries of fear; there is terror and no peace. Now let me ask you a question: Do men give birth to babies? Then why do they stand there, ashen-faced, hands pressed against their sides like a woman in labor? In all history there has never been such a time of terror. It will be a time of trouble for my people Israel. Yet in the end they will be saved! 'For in that day,' says the LORD of Heaven's Armies, 'I will break the yoke from their necks and snap their chains. Foreigners will no longer be their masters. For my people will serve the LORD their God and their king descended from David—the king I will raise up for them'" (Jeremiah 30:5-9).

A NEW KINGDOM WILL COMPLETE THE RETURN

The final return will not be completed until Christ returns to intervene as judge of the nations and the promised King to restore David's throne. The prophecies concerning the return, so dramatically begun in our history, will not be completed until all living Jews (drastically reduced in number during the Great Tribulation) are finally established in the Promised Land for a millennium of both peace and prosperity. Many of the Old Testament prophets, such as Ezekiel, Isaiah, Daniel, and Micah, echoed similar visions of this period.

Jeremiah prophesied the judgment that would fall on the non-

Jewish nations and then reported the message from the God of Israel in these words:

> But I will gather together the remnant of my flock from the countries where I have driven them. I will bring them back to their own sheepfold, and they will be fruitful and increase in number. Then I will appoint responsible shepherds who will care for them, and they will never be afraid again. Not a single one will be lost or missing. I, the LORD have spoken! "For the time is coming," says the LORD, "when I will raise up a righteous descendant from King David's line. He will be a King who rules with wisdom. He will do what is just and right throughout the land. And this will be his name: 'The LORD Is Our Righteousness.' In that day Judah will be saved, and Israel will live in safety. (Jeremiah 23:3-6)

Ezekiel's prophecy makes it clear that this will finally be accomplished immediately after a period of judgment and that the completion of the return will bring every living Jew into the land: "Then my people will know that I am the LORD their God, because I sent them away to exile and brought them home again. I will leave none of my people behind" (Ezekiel 39:28).

The present return of Israel to the land sets the stage for an important series of end-time events. Prophecies clearly predicted that Israel would be reestablished as a nation before the end of the period of the Gentiles. But non-Jewish nations were described as still in control of the destiny of Israel during a final hour of judgment and suffering. Jesus predicted, "They will be killed by the sword or sent away as captives to all the nations of the world. And Jerusalem will be trampled down by the Gentiles until the period of the Gentiles comes to an end" (Luke 21:24).

The next dramatic moves will involve the continued struggle for control of Jerusalem and the return of a portion of the land to the Palestinian Arabs as already witnessed in the Israeli withdrawal from Gaza in 2005. This struggle will become increasingly explosive because of the five million Palestinians dispossessed. Many have been forced to live as refugees and exiles in surrounding Arab states. Palestinian guerilla groups spawned from the refugee camps have pursued a strategy of terror and have made it difficult for moderate Arabs to negotiate compromise solutions.

Arab leaders have managed an uneasy alliance with the Palestinians that has often exploded in violence. In October 1974 the Arab summit conference at Rabat offered a solution for the sake of unity. The occupied West Bank of the Jordan was to become an independent Palestinian state run by the Palestine Liberation Organization (PLO). A government in exile was to be formed by early 1975 to prepare for negotiation with Israel.

The West Bank was originally conquered in the War of 1967 and, from Israel's point of view, is a legitimate possession of Israel. Israel continued to plant new settlements and the Palestinians continued to resist. Much of the world, however, including the United States, is putting pressure on Israel to turn the West Bank and the Gaza strip into an independent Palestinian state separate from Israel. This is the gist of the so-called "Road Map" for peace. However, the road map was tattered and torn after the stunning victory by Hamas in the Palestinian parliamentary election in January 2006. Initial exit polling indicated that the ruling Fatah Party had secured a fairly safe majority. But the next morning the world awoke to the stunning news that the Islamic terrorist group Hamas had won a landslide victory, securing 76 of 132 seats in the parliamentary elections. Fatah, the party of Palestinian Authority president Mahmoud Abbas, claimed a mere 43 seats.

TERRORISM AND THE NEED FOR PEACE

Hamas's support from Arab states and Iran will continue to be a thorn in Israel's side and create the ever-present threat of a terrorist war of attrition, by which they attempt to slowly wear down the Israelis through constant friction and harassment. Israel's economic resources are consumed and combatants and civilians are killed with no clear gains or victory. Cease-fires and peace negotiations are only attempts to gain advantage and continue the conflict.

Reaction around the world to the Hamas victory was swift and severe. America has said that it will not deal with Hamas unless they change their charter, which boldly calls for the destruction of Israel. Western nations threatened to cut off financial support to the Palestinian Authority as long as Hamas is in power, so Iran soon pledged $50 million to the Hamas-led government in Palestine.

On June 25, 2006, Hamas terrorists, using a system of tunnels, attacked an Israeli military outpost. They killed two soldiers, wounded three others, and kidnapped a sixth Israeli soldier. This sparked a fierce response from Israel. Then, on July 12, Hezbollah terrorists, in an almost identical attack, came across Israel's northern border from Lebanon, killing several Israeli soldiers and kidnapping two others. This second attack erupted into a thirty-four-day war during which Israel hit Hezbollah targets in southern Lebanon and was pummeled day after day by thousands of rockets and missiles supplied by Iran.

When one connects the dots, in fact, it's clear that Iran was behind these attacks. Iran is currently enriching uranium and threatening to annihilate Israel. If Iran obtains nuclear weapons, the missiles landing on Israel in the future could be armed with nuclear warheads. Israel's fierce reaction to the kidnapping of the two soldiers by Hezbollah could have been motivated by Israel's knowledge that a preemptive strike against Iran's nuclear facilities is inevitable. Weakening Hezbollah may have been an important first step in Israel's overall strategy for dealing with its greatest threat—Iran.

Terrorists now openly control the Palestinian government. Hamas, Hezbollah, terrorist attacks, reprisals, or Iran's nuclear ambitions could easily push the Middle East into open warfare. As moderate Arabs and European allies consolidate wealth and power, a forced settlement may be the only solution. New leaders will emerge to promise just such a peace. Israel's willingness in August 2006 to turn over southern Lebanon to a European-led peacekeeping force could easily be a prelude or first step in Israel's acceptance of a treaty that guarantees peace. With the threat of escalating terror and a disruption of the West's oil supply, the pressure for a "superimposed peace" will lead to the formation of the most vicious world empire of all time.

 See how today's headlines relate to this chapter at *http://www.prophecyhotline.com.*

CHAPTER 5

THE DECLINE AND FALL OF AMERICA

EVENT #4: American power and influence in the Middle East fade as the United States retreats to deal with the energy crisis and problems at home.

The average age of the world's greatest civilizations from the beginning of history has been about 200 years. During those 200 years, these nations always progressed through the following sequence:

From bondage to spiritual faith;
From spiritual faith to great courage;
From courage to liberty;
From liberty to abundance;
From abundance to complacency;
From complacency to apathy;
From apathy to dependence;
From dependence back into bondage.

COMMONLY ATTRIBUTED TO ALEXANDER FRASER TYTLER

I think that a lot of [Americans] are carrying around in their heads, unarticulated and even in some cases unnoticed, a sense that the wheels are coming off the trolley and the trolley off the tracks. . . . That our pollsters are preoccupied with "right track" and "wrong track" but missing the number of people who think the answer to "How are things going in America?" is "Off the tracks and hurtling forward, toward an unknown destination."

PEGGY NOONAN, OCTOBER 27, 2005

WHAT IS THE PLACE OF America in end-time prophecy? In the last one hundred years, the United States has become one of the most powerful and influential nations in all of history. Following the breakup of the Soviet Union, it became the only superpower in the world. Does the Bible have anything to say about the future of the United States?

The ancient prophets were primarily concerned with the Holy Land and its immediate neighbors. For this reason, it's not surprising that geographic areas remote from this center of biblical interest do not figure largely in prophecy and may not be mentioned at all. No specific mention of the United States or any other country in North or South America can be found in the Bible. Also, none of the rather obscure references to distant lands can be taken specifically as a reference to the United States. Therefore, any final, conclusive answer to the question of America's role in the end times is impossible. The prophetic timetable does point to some general conclusions about the role of the United States in end-time events, however.

THE WORLD SITUATION AT THE END TIME

The Bible provides an outline of major stages after the Rapture of the church: (1) a period of preparation, (2) the peace treaty that begins the seven-year tribulation period, and (3) the rise of the Antichrist, who will declare himself world ruler and break the peace treaty, beginning the time of Jacob's trouble. This will usher in the terrible judgments of the last three and a half years of the period of the Gentiles.

1. **Preparation.** Immediately after the Rapture there will be a period of preparation in which a group of ten world leaders will consolidate the power of the West and will emerge on the world stage. This ruling group or oligarchy will unite the European and Mediterranean countries into a new revived and powerful Western coalition like the Roman Empire. This is the iron fist that will stop the chaos.

2. **The peace treaty.** At the conclusion of this period of preparation, "a ruler will arise" (Daniel 9:26), the head of the Group of Ten, and will make a seven-year covenant with Israel (Daniel 9:27). This treaty will introduce a period of protection and peace for Israel by the leader who will later declare himself world ruler. The "small horn" of Daniel 7:8 will be revealed as the coming world dictator who will take over the power consolidated by the Group of Ten. This marks the beginning of what is generally described as the last week of Daniel's seventy weeks of years—the seven-year tribulation period.

3. **The world dictator.** The world leader will break his covenant with Israel after three and a half years. He will declare himself world dictator and assume the prerogatives of deity. He will declare himself god and will use the new demonic world religion to fool many. These rapid-fire events will usher in the Great Tribulation with its corresponding period of persecution for Israel. This three-and-a-half-year period will end with the gathering of rebelling armies moving toward Israel to begin the Battle of Armageddon.

Although the Scriptures do not give any clear word concerning the role of the United States in relation to the revived Roman Empire, it is clear this will be a consolidation of the power of the West. Unlike the coalitions led by the United States, this coalition will be led by others—the Group of Ten.

It is very likely that the United States will be in some form of alliance with this coalition whose power is centered in Europe and the Middle East. Most citizens of the United States of America have come from Europe, and their sympathies would more naturally be with a European alliance than with Russia or countries in eastern Asia. It may even be that the United States will provide large support for the Group of Ten as it will seem to be opposed to Iran, Russia, Asia, and Africa.

Actually a balance of power in the world may exist at that time that's very similar to the present world situation; namely, Europe and America may be in formal alliance with Israel in opposition to the radical Islamic countries of the Middle East, as well as Russia and China. Based on geographic, religious, and economic factors, such an alliance of powers seems a natural sequence of the polarization of nations in a tug-of-war over the Middle East and its resources.

NO LONGER A SUPERPOWER

What is perfectly clear is that the world dictator will lead the only superpower in the world by the middle of the great tribulation period (Revelation 13:7). Even if the United States has an alliance with the revived Roman Empire, something will have happened to the United States' role as the world's policeman. It will simply drop out as a superpower. The end-time events do not include America as the great international superpower it was at the beginning of the twenty-first century.

But what could reduce America to a subordinate role as ten Western leaders consolidate the West's political, economic, and military power? What kind of event could bring America to her knees? At least four possibilities, which fit the current world situation, could occur alone or in a fatal combination.

1. **Terrorist attack**. First, some maintain that the total absence of any scriptural reference to America in the end time is evidence that the United States will have been crippled by a nuclear attack, weapons of mass destruction, or some other major catastrophe. If that were the case the United States would no longer be a major player in international affairs. In the post-9/11 world the detonation of a dirty bomb, nuclear device, or biological weapon on U.S. soil is a dreaded yet distinct possibility. Such an attack could kill millions of people, cripple the economy, and reduce the United States to a second-rate power overnight.

2. The "break point" in oil. The second event that could demote the United States from superpower status would be reaching the break point in oil. Such a break point will be reached when the oil crisis finally peaks and the entire world energy complex scrambles to rebalance itself, stake out energy claims, and adjust to the new situation. According to some experts, this point may be reached in the next decade. If the United States is still dependent on imported oil when this occurs, America will enter the uncharted waters of a new era of uncertainty and volatility.[1]

Iran, the world's fourth leading exporter of oil, has promised the United States "harm and pain" if it takes any serious action against Iran's nuclear ambitions. Part of this harm and pain might come in reduced oil exports that could strangle the West with a dramatic rise in oil prices. Though America does not import any oil from Iran, any substantial reduction in the world's oil supply anywhere in the world will cause the price of oil to escalate dramatically on world markets.

If the oil break point is reached without sufficient preparation, U.S. national security would be compromised. The U.S. military machine runs on oil—lots of oil. Without it, America cannot exert its power on the world stage. In this scenario, all available fuel would have to be conserved and diverted to protect our nation. Strategic energy reserves would quickly dry up if the oil supply from the Middle East were disrupted. If oil from the Middle East stopped abruptly, trucks that transport necessary food, medicines, and the necessities of life would compete for meager resources. Nonmilitary aircraft would immediately face severe cutbacks in aviation fuel. Normal commercial traffic would come to a screeching halt. The U.S. economy would go into full cardiac arrest.

The world is entering the long dark tunnel of a new energy era. Only God knows what's at the end of the tunnel for our world and for America. The unquenchable thirst for oil may lead to America's downfall.

3. **A fall from within.** Third, history records how many great nations have risen to unusual power and influence only to decline because of internal corruption, compromise, and a collapse of political will. It may well be that the United States today is at the zenith of its power much as Babylon was in the sixth century BC prior to its sudden downfall at the hands of the Medes and the Persians (Daniel 5).

Any realistic survey of moral conditions in the world today would justify a judgment of God on any nation, including the United States. The long-suffering God has offered unusual benefits to the United States, both in political and religious freedom and economic blessing. But it could be argued that America has squandered its birthright and that judgment is long overdue. The question no longer is whether America deserves judgment, but rather why divine judgment has been so long withheld from a wasteful nation that is blessed so abundantly.

A partial answer to this question may be that the United States has been a major source of Christian testimony in the world. Although the United States represents only about 5 percent of the total world population, in the last century many of the missionaries and much of the money spent on world evangelism have come from America. God's major purpose in this present age is to call people to faith in Christ and to have the gospel preached to all nations. The prosperity America has enjoyed is God's blessing and is intended to be used in spreading Christianity to the ends of the earth.

Another important reason for delay in divine judgment upon America is the Abrahamic promise concerning his seed, "I will bless those who bless you and curse those who treat you with contempt" (Genesis 12:3). For the most part, the United States has been a defender of the Jewish people. In America, descendants of Abraham have enjoyed religious freedom and the opportunity to create wealth. Judgment on other nations has frequently been preceded by anti-Semitism and open hostility or persecution of the Jewish people. In the United States, Jewish people have enjoyed opportunity and freedom from persecution. The political influence of both the Jewish and evangelical communities has guaranteed that the United States remains a staunch ally of the nation of Israel.

4. **The Rapture reason.** The fourth possible explanation for America's absence in the end times is the Rapture of the church. It's clear that if Christ came for His church and all true Christians were taken out of this world, America would be weakened and perilously crippled. While America is not the Christian nation many people envision, America has more believers in Jesus Christ per capita than any other nation.[2] If the Rapture was to happen today, the true church would suddenly be gone, and America would experience a significant loss of leaders and citizens in all walks of life. The Rapture of the church would seriously disrupt the U.S. economy, government, and military forces.

Moreover, when the Rapture occurs, America's missionary endeavors will come to an abrupt halt. It is very likely that America will immediately withdraw her support of Israel. The drastically changed situation could alter God's material and political blessing upon the United States. If God's purpose for the United States is to build His church, evangelize the world, and protect Israel, America may no longer be the fortunate recipient of God's blessing or protection after the Rapture.

In all probability the decline of the United States will result from the impact of not one but several events that combine to make the

United States withdraw from the role of superpower and world police-man. The U.S. intervention in Afghanistan and Iraq has proven that playing the role of world policeman is a difficult, bloody, and impossible task.

When the United States abandons its unilateral role as the most dominant power in the world, the balance of power will shift quickly to Europe and the Middle East. One or more of the possible scenarios described above could seriously weaken the U.S. economy and turn America's attention to itself and provoke a national mood of isolationism in world affairs.

AMERICA'S TIME IS SHORT

Although any conclusion about the role of America in the end times is necessarily tentative, the scriptural evidence is sufficient to conclude that America in that day will not be a superpower and apparently will not figure largely in either the political, economic, or religious leadership of the world.

Yet in view of the imminent return of the Lord, Christians in the United States—and around the world—should remember that the cause of evangelism is urgent. If prophecy has any one message for this generation, it's that time and opportunity are short. Impending world conditions soon may close the door for further witness in many areas. What is true of America is true for the evangelical church throughout the world. The prophetic timetable serves to emphasize the importance of the present task of spreading the gospel, beginning at Jerusalem and to the uttermost parts of the world.

The destiny of nations is in the hands of the omnipotent God. Every nation is "under God." History is moving inexorably to its prophesied consummation as the nations of the world take their places to act out the drama of predicted end-time events. The divine program in all its detail will be fulfilled. The world will rush to judgment. The Son of God will reign in Zion. The nations will bow at His feet. Ultimately the present earth will be replaced with a new heaven and a new earth in which the new Jerusalem will be the home of the redeemed of all ages. The elect of all nations will continue throughout eternity to worship and adore the infinite triune God whose majesty, wisdom, and power will be unquestioned. In that eternal day, God's love and grace will be supremely revealed in those among all nations who have been redeemed by the blood of the Lamb.

See how today's headlines relate to this chapter at *http://www.prophecyhotline.com.*

CHAPTER 6

THE NEW
PAX ROMANA

EVENT #5: To save Western civilization from total collapse, the "Group of Ten" world leaders create an iron fist to stop the chaos and assure the supply of oil to the West.

Any peace, even the most inequitable, should be preferred to the most righteous war.

CICERO

We must build a kind of United States of Europe.

WINSTON CHURCHILL

At the dawn of the twenty-first century, a geopolitical revolution of historic dimensions is under way across the Atlantic: the unification of Europe. Twenty-five nations have joined together—with another dozen or so on the waiting list—to build a common economy, government, and culture. Europe is a more integrated place today than at any time since the Roman Empire.

T. R. REID, *THE UNITED STATES OF EUROPE*

NO MATTER HOW ONE LOOKS at it, the world today is a more dangerous place than at any time in history. Nuclear weapons in the wrong hands could wreak catastrophic, apocalyptic havoc. Terror attacks threaten to cut the oil supply line to Western nations that depend on Middle East oil for the survival of their economies. Michael Klare, an expert in global politics, observes, "Regional conflict, civil war, insurgency, terrorism—these are the most persistent and widespread threats to the global flow of petroleum in the early twenty-first century."[1]

How long can the world tolerate this explosive situation with hostages, terrorist attacks, the escalating Middle East crisis, the proliferation of nuclear weapons, disrupted oil supplies, and the daily threat of war?

The only real solution is a peace treaty that settles disputes, disarms the antagonists, and provides absolute guarantees. In short, a peace treaty backed up by force. A powerful leader will seize world attention by such an offer when the world is on the brink of chaos. He will give the world what it wants. He will bring terror under control, guarantee the flow of oil, and temporarily diffuse the time bomb in the Middle East.

PEACE AND THE FINAL COUNTDOWN

A peace settlement in the Middle East is one of the most important events predicted for the end times. The signing of this peace treaty will start the final seven-year countdown leading to Armageddon and introduce the new world leader who will be destined to become world dictator—the infamous Antichrist.

According to Daniel 9:27, the last seven years leading up to the second coming of Christ will begin with just such a peace settlement. The same passage describes a covenant to be made between the nation of Israel and the ruler who will rise to power (Daniel 9:26), who is related to the Roman Empire and the people who destroyed Jerusalem in AD 70. While the details of the covenant are not given, it will be an attempt to settle the Arab-Israeli controversy that has focused world attention on the Middle East. It will promise to stop terrorism and stabilize the world economy. It may take the form of a forced peace settlement in which Israel returns the land conquered through war in exchange for strong international guarantees for Israel's safety and abundance.

Scriptures describe a world situation not unlike what we have today preceding such a peace settlement. First there will be an alignment of ten leaders who emerge to protect the interests of the West. In Daniel 7:7 and 7:24 this is symbolized by ten horns on a beast that represents the last world empire, the Roman Empire in its final and revised form. Many interpreters of biblical prophecy have felt that the European Union will be a fulfillment of this predicted alignment of nations. The European Union is the preliminary form or at least the forerunner of this ten-leader group. The final power block initially led by the Group of Ten will constitute the revived Roman Empire, which will have the economic and political power necessary to control Europe. The final leader to emerge must eventually be able to seize control of three of the ten leaders and create a consolidation of power very much like the Roman Empire of the past (Daniel 7:8).

THE MARCH OF EMPIRES

About 2,500 years ago the Jewish prophet Daniel was given a panoramic revelation by God that revealed the sweep of world history from Daniel's day all the way up to the second coming of Jesus back to planet earth. His timeless prophecy is as relevant today as the day it was written. Events we see happening today strikingly foreshadow his ancient message.

Daniel wrote most of his great prophecy in the middle of the sixth century BC, near the end of the seventy-year Jewish exile in Babylon. During this time of discipline by God, He knew that His people would have all kinds of questions. They were no doubt asking questions such as—Is God finished with us? Will God be faithful to His covenant with Abraham to give us the land of Israel forever? Will the Kingdom promised to David ever be realized? Will the Messiah ever come to rule and reign over the earth?

In Daniel 2 and 7 God encouraged His people and answered their questions by giving them an overview of the course of world history. God wanted them to know that His promises were sure and that He would keep His Word—that the promised Kingdom would eventually come to Israel. However, God also wanted them to know that the Kingdom would not come immediately. Before the King and His Kingdom would come, four great world empires would rule over Israel in succession. With the benefit of twenty-twenty hindsight we now know that these four empires were Babylon, Medo-Persia, Greece, and Rome.

In Daniel 2 these four empires are pictured as four metals in a great statue that King Nebuchadnezzar saw in a dream. In Daniel 7 these same world empires are pictured as four great wild beasts rising up out of the Mediterranean Sea.

Up to this point almost everyone is in general agreement about the meaning of Nebuchadnezzar's dream in Daniel 2 and Daniel's night vision in Daniel 7. But in Daniel 2 the final form of the Roman Empire is pictured by the feet of iron and baked clay and the ten toes on the image. Likewise in Daniel 7, the final phase of the Roman Empire is depicted by the ten horns on the terrifying beast. These ten toes and ten horns are identified as ten kings (Daniel 2:44; 7:24). Yet we know from history that the Roman Empire never existed in a ten-king form as required by both Daniel 2 and 7.

Moreover, there is a complete, sudden destruction of the great image in Daniel 2 and the beast in Daniel 7. But the Roman Empire gradually deteriorated and declined until the western part of the empire fell in AD 476 and the eastern leg was cut off in AD 1453. A more gradual process could hardly be imagined. With its slow decline, the Roman Empire left unfulfilled the sudden destruction of the feet of the image and the ten-horn stage of the beast in Daniel 7:7.

INTERPRETING THE FUTURE IN LIGHT OF THE PAST

The principal reason for believing in the revival of the ancient Roman Empire is the simple fact that prophecy requires it. Prophecies dealing

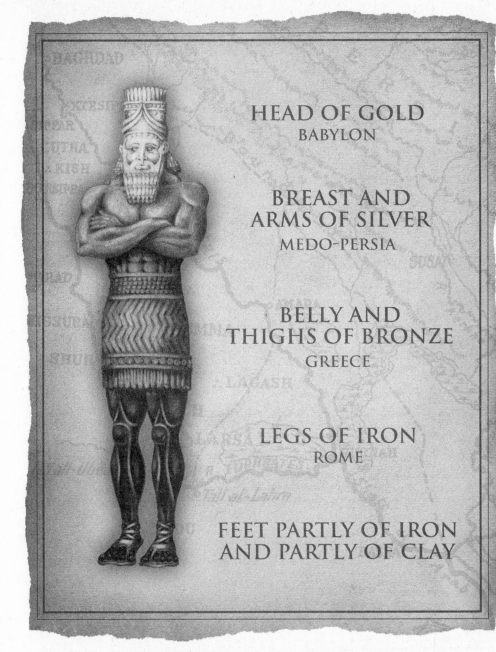

HEAD OF GOLD
BABYLON

BREAST AND
ARMS OF SILVER
MEDO-PERSIA

BELLY AND
THIGHS OF BRONZE
GREECE

LEGS OF IRON
ROME

FEET PARTLY OF IRON
AND PARTLY OF CLAY

with the final phase of this empire have not been literally fulfilled like the prophecies of the first three world empires. To those who believe the Bible, the prophecies of the future are just as authentic as the prophecies already fulfilled in the history of past world empires. One must conclude that a revival of the ancient Roman Empire in the form anticipated in the unfulfilled prophecies of Daniel is yet to appear on the stage of world history.

The future form of the Roman Empire according to Daniel will emerge prior to the coming of Christ to rule and reign over the earth. This future manifestation will take the form of a coalition or confederation of ten world leaders (symbolized by the ten toes in Daniel 2 and the ten horns in Daniel 7) that will encompass the same basic geographical territory as the original or historical Roman Empire.

In presenting these two forms of the Roman Empire, Daniel skips over many centuries from historical Rome immediately to end-time prophecy. This kind of "prophetic skip" is consistent with a principle found in much of Old Testament prophecy: Often the writer describes events that were prophetically fulfilled in Israel's exile or the first coming of Christ and then moves almost immediately from those details into end-time prophecy, describing the Great Tribulation and millennial reign of Christ. (See, for example, Isaiah 9:6-7; Daniel 9:26-27; Zechariah 9:9-10; Malachi 3:1-3.)

The end-time ten-king form of the Roman Empire is pictured in Daniel 2 as the ten toes on the great metallic image and in Daniel 7 as ten horns on the fourth or terrible beast. The chart below shows the parallels between Daniel 2 and 7, especially in the final phase of the Roman Empire.

Comparison of Daniel 2 and Daniel 7

WORLD EMPIRE	DANIEL 2	DANIEL 7
Babylon	Head of Gold	Lion
Medo-Persia	Chest and Arms of Silver	Bear
Greece	Belly and Thighs of Bronze	Leopard
Rome	Legs of Iron	Terrifying Beast
Revived Rome	Ten Toes	Ten Horns
Empire of the Antichrist		Little Horn

THREE FUTURE STAGES OF THE ROMAN EMPIRE

It appears that the future, revived Roman Empire will go through three stages. First, a group of ten kings or some form of a ruling oligarchy within the ancient Roman Empire will appear, described here as the Group of Ten. This will mark the first phase of its revival. Second, a strong man will emerge who will consolidate these ten nations into a united empire and probably extend its borders in various directions. Third, there is the final stage of the revived Roman Empire when, by declaration or edict, its power extends to the entire earth. The Antichrist will simply declare he is ruler of the world in the power vacuum created by the destruction of the armies of Gog and Magog described in Ezekiel 38–39. The final or third stage may be in a state of partial disintegration at the time of the second coming of Christ since it appears that there is warfare and rebellion against the new, self-declared world ruler at the end of the Great Tribulation.

It's probable that the revived Roman Empire will include nations from Europe and possibly even from northern Africa and some nations from western Asia, since the revived Roman Empire to some extent is viewed as including the three preceding empires that were largely Asiatic. As the Holy Land is the center of biblical interest, it would only be natural for the empire to include this area, especially when one considers that the Holy Land became a part of the area of influence of the Roman Empire as demonstrated in the treaty with Israel (Daniel 9:27) and in the later warfare described as being in this area (Ezekiel 38–39; Daniel 11:40-45; Zechariah 14:1-3).

Although the specific identity of the ten kings, or world leaders, can't be determined at this time, there has been much speculation concerning the materials that form the toes of the image described in Daniel 2:41-43. They are described as being partly of iron and partly of pottery or dried clay. In the prophecy attention is called to the fact that iron does not mix with the clay and therefore that the feet of the image are the weakest portion of the entire structure. According to Daniel 2:41-43, "The feet and toes you saw were a combination of iron and baked clay, showing that this kingdom will be divided. Like iron mixed with clay, it will have some of the strength of iron. But while some parts of it will be as strong as iron, other parts will be as weak as clay. This mixture of iron and clay also shows that these kingdoms will try to strengthen themselves by forming alliances with each other through intermarriage. But they will not hold together, just as iron and clay do not mix."

It is clear that since the legs of iron represent the strength of the ancient Roman Empire, the clay must in some sense denote the idea of political weakness or instability. The best interpretation is that the clay mixed with iron represents the diverse racial, religious, or political elements that are included in the confines of this final revived Roman Empire that contribute to its ultimate downfall. This view is supported by the fact that the revived Roman Empire, when it does reach its world stage, will immediately begin to encounter difficulties that result in the final world conflict, which is underway when Christ returns.

This mention of iron and clay, or inherent strength and weakness at the same time, is reflected in the European Union (EU) today. The EU has great economic and political clout, but its diversity in culture, language, and politics is also ever present. One can easily see how the EU could become the feet and toes of iron and clay.

E-UNIFICATION OF THE ROMAN EMPIRE

It appears that the revived Roman Empire described by Daniel is beginning to take shape. The reunification of the Roman Empire began officially in 1957 with a treaty appropriately named "The Treaty (or Treaties) of Rome." This treaty was signed on March 25, 1957, on Capitoline Hill, which is one of the famous Seven Hills of Rome. Gradually, yet steadily since then, the nations of Europe have come together one by one. Amazingly, this amalgamation of nations has taken only about fifty years.

The addition of ten new nations to the EU on May 1, 2004, brought the total number of members to twenty-five. These nations brought

75 million people into the EU, expanding the population of the EU to 450 million people and surpassing North America as the world's biggest economic zone. On January 1, 2007, two more nations, Romania and Bulgaria, were admitted to the European Union.

At least two key events in the twentieth century provided the necessary impetus for the reuniting of Europe, which was the core of the historical Roman Empire. First, there were two world wars. For centuries the nations of Europe fought one another again and again. But in the aftermath of World War II, a dramatic change occurred. Instead of building up for the next great armed conflict as they had done for centuries, they decided to come together in a coalition of nations that was originally called the Common Market. For the first time in 1,600 years the necessary preconditions for a reunited, revived Roman Empire predicted by Daniel were in place. This situation establishes, at least on the surface, a peaceful relationship between these major countries. This is a necessary prelude to the revival of the Roman Empire as prophesied in the Bible.

Second, the dissolution of the Soviet Union paved the way for the rise of the revived Roman Empire. The eight Eastern European nations that joined the EU in 2004 could never have joined it as long as the Soviet bloc was still in power. So, the fall of the Soviet empire in 1991 was another necessary development that set the stage for the revival of the Roman Empire.

Economic self-interest, national security, and the threat of international terrorism in Europe and the Middle East point to the necessity for an alliance of nations to bring peace and economic prosperity to the region. Changes necessary to make the situation conform to the prophetic anticipation of Daniel could take place rapidly in the present world scene.

BACK TOGETHER AGAIN

The Roman Empire that had ceased to exist for 1,600 years appears to be coming back together before our eyes. The EU today has a 732-member parliament; a parliament building in Strasbourg, France; a presidency that rotates among the member nations every six months; a supreme court; committees; and one currency that has been approved by thirteen of the twenty-seven member nations and is currently in circulation. The EU allows unrestricted travel for citizens among member nations, and it is presently working toward a unified military and criminal justice system.

What has developed in Europe during the last fifty years looks strikingly similar to what the Bible predicts for the end times. The basic governmental and economic components are in place for some kind of ten-ruler group or committee to come on the scene in the EU and ascend to power. And the next step will be for one man to rise to ultimate power in that group and take over as the strongman to rule the world. That man will be the Antichrist, and he will rule over the final form of the Roman Empire and ultimately the whole world.

While the current EU is not the final, ultimate fulfillment of the biblical prophecies, the events in Europe today seem to be the necessary prelude to the reunited Roman Empire prophesied by Daniel over 2,500 years ago.

The stage is set for a new alignment of power similar to the revived Roman Empire, which will promise peace to a world disrupted by catastrophe and on the brink of chaos.

HOW MUCH LONGER?

What form will the coming peace settlement take? In view of the many surprises in the Middle East, it is hazardous to guess the precise form of such a final peace settlement. It is also difficult to predict what catastrophic events will make this forced peace necessary. Will it be the economic chaos created by the oil breaking point with soaring prices and disruption of supply? Will it be a new outbreak of all-out war with chemical weapons or use of tactical nuclear weapons? Will it be a sudden escalation in the Middle East crisis? Whatever the reason, the world must be in danger of self-destruction or Israel and the nations of the world would not surrender power to the new leaders of the revived Roman Empire.

Whatever the precipitating events or the form of the peace agreement, ultimately it must give Israel security from attack and freedom from the constant state of military defense. It is very possible that an international peacekeeping force and secure boundaries may be guaranteed by the new and powerful Group of Ten. A general disarmament in the area may also be part of the agreement. In the aftermath of Israel's indecisive war with Hezbollah, Israel was willing to allow a peacekeeping force, led by EU forces, to guarantee the security of its northern border. Israel's agreement to have a U.N. peacekeeping force control southern Lebanon could be a prelude to its willingness to give over more and more of its security to the West.

The key issue in negotiations will be the city of Jerusalem itself, which Israel prizes more than any other possession. Undoubtedly there will be a strong attempt to maintain Jerusalem as an international city, with free access not only for Jews, but for Christians and Muslims as well. The Temple area may be internationalized, and Israel's territorial conquests will be greatly reduced.

With the rise of radical Islamic terrorism and the changing role of the United States as the sole supporting force behind Israel's continuity as a nation, it seems that any settlement that does not deal with Jerusalem will not satisfy the Arab world.

How soon will such a peace settlement come? No one can predict. But come it must—here the Scriptures are emphatic. There will be a treaty between the new world leader and Israel (Daniel 9:27) that will permit Israel to continue and to renew her religious ceremonies, including the building of a Jewish Temple and the reactivation of Jewish sacrifices. All of this was anticipated in the prophecies of Daniel 9:27 and 12:11 and was implied in the prophecy of Christ Himself relating to the stopping of the sacrifices when the treaty is broken (Matthew 24:15).

Made to Be Broken

How will Hamas, Hezbollah, other Islamic extremists, and Iran ever negotiate a settlement of any kind when they do not recognize Israel's right to exist? After the Israel-Hezbollah war in the summer of 2006, we can see how the Middle East situation can rapidly deteriorate, requiring a strong military presence to restore order. Or perhaps a peace settlement will be accepted by these nations to give them a temporary position of advantage in preparation for a possible later war with Israel.

Unfortunately, the final peace will only be a temporary consolidation of the world leaders' military and economic power—it will be a peace made to be broken. The peace settlement prophesied in Scripture will be a bid for world recognition by the new leader of the revived Roman Empire. The peace will be observed for only three and a half years and will be a major stepping-stone in his rise to world power. The peace settlement will be destined to be broken, bringing devastating consequences for the world and terrible persecution for Israel. This breaking of the treaty will commence what Christ described as "greater anguish than at any time since the world began. And it will never be so great again" (Matthew 24:21). Jeremiah referred to this period as "a time of trouble for my people Israel" (Jeremiah 30:7).

Waiting for the Prince of Peace

The final persecution of Jews during their time of trouble will awaken Israel's understanding about what has taken place. All the hopes and illusions of the past will be stripped away. This clear fulfillment of prophecy will lead to the startling realization that the first coming of the Messiah is past and that His second coming is near. In the anguish of the last three and a half years of the time of horror, Jewish believers from this period will cling to the hope of Christ's second coming. Jesus prophesied that He would not come again until Israel would say, "Blessings on the one who comes in the name of the LORD!" (Matthew 23:39).

See how today's headlines relate to this chapter at
http://www.prophecyhotline.com.

CHAPTER 7

THE RUSSIAN-ISLAMIC INVASION OF ISRAEL

EVENT #6: In response to the "Group of Ten," a new alliance of Islamic nations and Russia challenges the West, attacks Israel, and is destroyed.

> Would it be a difficult military option? Sure, it would be a difficult military option. But you cannot remove it from the table. I think we could have Armageddon.
>
> SENATOR JOHN MCCAIN, *MEET THE PRESS*, APRIL 2, 2006

> "CNN has received unconfirmed reports that Russian and coalition forces in Lebanon are beginning to advance toward the Israeli border. Israel radio is reporting that a column of some five hundred Russian and Iranian battle tanks is heading south from Beirut and is expected to link up with another two thousand tanks positioned just east of Tyre and Sidon." . . . He knew the prophecy cold by now. He knew what was coming next. The judgment of Russia. The destruction of radical Islam. The realignment of nations and fortunes, unprecedented in human history.
>
> JOEL ROSENBERG, *THE EZEKIEL OPTION* (A NOVEL)

ONE OF THE GREAT EVENTS of the end times is an invasion of Israel by a vast horde of nations from every direction. This invasion, which is known as the Battle of Gog and Magog, is graphically described in Ezekiel 38–39. Taken literally, it predicts a last days invasion of Israel from every direction by a vast horde of nations and God's direct, supernatural intervention to annihilate the invaders. Events in our world today strikingly foreshadow this coming invasion. These nations, which will not be a part of the Group of Ten, will act independently of the world dictator.

To help us gain a clear understanding of Ezekiel 38–39—two riveting chapters—and how current events point toward their fulfillment, we will use the standard questions of journalism: who, where, when, why, what, and how.

THE PARTICIPANTS (EZEKIEL 38:1-7): WHO?

The prophecy of the battle of Gog and Magog begins with a list of ten proper names in Ezekiel 38:1-7, or what we might call God's Most Wanted List:

> And the word of the LORD came to me saying, "Son of man, set your face toward Gog of the land of Magog, the prince of Rosh, Meshech and Tubal, and prophesy against him and say, 'Thus says the Lord GOD, "Behold, I am against you, O Gog, prince of Rosh, Meshech and Tubal. I will turn you about and put hooks into your jaws, and I will bring you out, and all your army, horses and horsemen, all of them splendidly attired, a great company with buckler and shield, all of them wielding swords; Persia, Ethiopia and Put with them, all of them with shield and helmet; Gomer with all its troops; Beth-togarmah from the remote parts of the north with all its troops—many peoples with you. Be prepared, and prepare yourself, you and all your companies that are assembled about you, and be a guard for them." (Ezekiel 38:1-7, NASB)

The name *Gog*, which occurs eleven times in Ezekiel 38–39, is a name or title of the leader of the invasion. It is clear that Gog is an individual since he is directly addressed several times by God (38:14; 39:1) and since he is called a prince and ruler (38:2; 39:1, NASB). The Group of Ten's bold move to consolidate absolute power over the Middle East will result in a disastrous countermove by Gog, the military leader of a coalition of Islamic nations and Russia.

The other nine proper names in Ezekiel 38:1-7 are specific geographical locations: Magog, Rosh, Meshech, Tubal, Persia, Cush (often translated as Ethiopia), Put, Gomer, and Beth-togarmah. None of the place names in Ezekiel 38:1-7 exist on any modern map. Ezekiel used ancient place names that were familiar to the people of his day. While the names of these geographical locations have changed many times throughout history and may change again, the geographical territory remains the same. Regardless of what names they may carry at the time of this invasion, it is these specific geographical areas that will be involved. Each of these ancient geographical locations from Ezekiel's day will be briefly examined, and the modern counterpart will be identified.[1]

Magog

The Jewish historian Josephus reported that the ancient Scythians inhabited the land of Magog.[2] These northern nomadic tribes inhabited land from Central Asia across the southern steppes of modern Russia. Magog today probably represents the former underbelly of the Soviet Union: Kazakhstan, Kyrgyzstan, Uzbekistan, Turkmenistan, and Tajikistan. Afghanistan could also be part of this territory. Each of these nations is dominated by Islam. Their combined population is in excess of ninety million.

Rosh

Bible scholars have often identified Rosh with Russia. But this conclusion has not been unanimous. There are two key issues that must be resolved to properly interpret Rosh in Ezekiel 38–39: (1) Is Rosh a common noun or a name? and (2) Does Rosh have any relation to Russia?

The first point that must be considered is whether the word *Rosh* in

Ezekiel 38:2-3 and 39:1 (NASB) is a proper name or simply a common noun. The word *rosh* in Hebrew simply means head, top, summit, or chief. It is a very common word that appears over six hundred times in the Old Testament.

Many translations render *rosh* as a common noun and translate it as the word *chief*. The King James Version, Revised Standard Version, English Standard Version, New American Bible, New Living Translation, and the New International Version all adopt this translation. However, the Jerusalem Bible, New English Bible, and New American Standard Bible all translate *Rosh* as a proper name indicating a geographical location.

The weight of evidence favors taking *Rosh* as a proper name in Ezekiel 38–39. There are five arguments that favor this view. First, the eminent Hebrew scholars C. F. Keil and Wilhelm Gesenius both hold that the better translation of *Rosh* in Ezekiel 38:2-3 and 39:1 is as a proper noun referring to a specific geographical location.[3]

Second, the Septuagint, which is the Greek translation of the Old Testament, translates *Rosh* as the proper name *Ros*. This is especially significant because the Septuagint was translated only three centuries after Ezekiel was written (obviously much closer to the original than any modern translation). The mistranslation of *Rosh* in many modern translations as an adjective can be traced to the Latin *Vulgate* of Jerome.[4]

Third, in their articles on *Rosh*, many Bible dictionaries and encyclopedias support taking it as a proper name in Ezekiel 38. Here are a few examples: *New Bible Dictionary, Wycliffe Bible Dictionary,* and *International Standard Bible Encyclopedia.*

Fourth, *Rosh* is mentioned the first time in Ezekiel 38:2 and then repeated in Ezekiel 38:3 and 39:1. If *Rosh* were simply a title, it would be dropped in these two places because when titles are repeated in Hebrew they are generally abbreviated.

Fifth, the most impressive evidence in favor of taking *Rosh* as a proper name is simply that this translation is the most accurate. G. A. Cooke translates Ezekiel 38:2, "the chief of Rosh, Meshech and Tubal."

He calls this "the most natural way of rendering the Hebrew."[5] The evidence of biblical scholarship implies that *Rosh* should be understood as a proper name, the name of a specific geographical area.

Having established that *Rosh* should be taken as a proper name of a geographical area, the next task is to determine what geographical location it refers to.

There are three key reasons for understanding Rosh in Ezekiel 38–39 as a reference to Russia. First, linguistically, there is evidence that *Rosh* is Russia. The great Hebrew scholar Wilhelm Gesenius noted in the nineteenth century that "Rosh is undoubtedly the Russians."[6]

Second, historically, there is substantial evidence that in Ezekiel's day there was a group of people known variously as Rash, Reshu, or Ros who lived in what today is southern Russia.[7]

Third, geographically, Ezekiel 38–39 emphasizes repeatedly that at least part of this invading force will come from the "distant north" (NLT) or the "remote parts of the north" (NASB). Biblical directions are usually given in reference to Israel, which on God's compass is the center of the earth (Ezekiel 38:12). If you draw a line directly north from Israel, the land that is most remote or distant to the north is Russia. Therefore, it seems very likely that Russia will be the leader of the Gog coalition.

Meshech and Tubal

Meshech and Tubal are normally mentioned together in Scripture. In his notes in *The Scofield Study Bible* for Ezekiel 38:2, C. I. Scofield identified Meshech and Tubal as the Russian cities of Moscow and Tobolsk. Scofield wrote, "That the primary reference is to the northern (European) powers, headed up by Russia, all agree. . . . The reference to Meshech and Tubal (Moscow and Tobolsk) is a clear mark of identification."

While the names do sound alike, this is not a proper method of identification. Meshech and Tubal are mentioned two other times in Ezekiel. In Ezekiel 27:13 they are mentioned as trading partners with ancient Tyre. In Ezekiel 32:26 their recent defeat is recorded. It is highly unlikely that ancient Tyre (modern Lebanon) was trading with Moscow and the Siberian city of Tobolsk. The preferred identification is that Meshech and Tubal are the ancient Moschoi and Tibarenoi in Greek writings or Tabal and Musku in Assyrian inscriptions. The ancient locations are in present-day Turkey. This is best understood as a reference to modern Turkey, an Islamic country. Current trends in Turkey appear to be moving the nation away from Europe back toward Russia and other Islamic nations.

Persia

The words *Persia*, *Persian*, or *Persians* are found thirty-five times in the Old Testament. In Ezekiel 38:5, Persia is best understood as modern-day Iran. The ancient land of Persia became the modern nation of Iran in March 1935, and then the name was changed to the Islamic Republic of Iran in 1979. Iran's present population is sixty-eight million. Iran's regime is the world's number one sponsor of terror. Iran is making its bid for regional supremacy at the same time it is pursuing nuclear weapons. The Iranian president has declared that Israel "must be wiped off the map." Clearly, modern Iran is a country hostile to Israel and the West. (It is even more of a threat to Israel because of the end-time beliefs of its president, an issue we'll examine in greater depth later in this chapter.)

Ethiopia (Cush)

The Hebrew word *Cush* in Ezekiel 38:5 is often translated Ethiopia in modern versions. Ancient Cush was called Kusu by the Assyrians and Babylonians, Kos or Kas by the Egyptians, and Nubia by the Greeks. Secular history locates Cush directly south of ancient Egypt extending down past the modern city of Khartoum, which is the capital of modern Sudan. Thus, modern Sudan inhabits the ancient land of Cush. Sudan is a hard-line Islamic nation that supported Iraq in the Gulf War and harbored Osama bin Laden from 1991 to 1996. It is not surprising that this part of Africa would be hostile to the West and could easily join in an attack on Israel.

Libya (Put)

Some ancient sources indicate that *Put* or *Phut* was a North African nation—with references documented in the Hebrew text footnotes in the New Living Translation for a number of passages, including Jeremiah 46:9 and Ezekiel 27:10; 30:5. The Babylonian Chronicles, a series of tablets recording ancient Babylonian history, indicate that Putu was the "distant" land west of Egypt, which would become modern-day Libya. The Septuagint, which was the Greek translation of the Old Testament, renders the word *Put* as Libues. Modern Libya is an Islamic nation that has been under the rule of Colonel Mu'ammar al-Gadhafi since 1969. Libya's recent attempt to placate the West does not change its allegiance to Islamic extremism and hatred of Israel.

Gomer

Gomer has often been identified by Bible teachers as Germany, or more particularly East Germany before the fall of communism. This identification is superficial and not the literal meaning of the word in its cultural and historic context.

Gomer is probably a reference to the ancient Cimmerians or *Kimmerioi*. Ancient history identifies biblical Gomer with the Akkadian Gi-mir-ra-a and the Armenian Gamir. Beginning in the eighth century BC the Cimmerians occupied territory in Anatolia, which is modern Turkey. Josephus noted that the Gomerites were identified with the Galatians who inhabited what today is central Turkey.[8] Turkey is an Islamic nation with deepening ties with Russia. Turkey's natural allegiance is not to the EU but to her Muslim neighbors. Turkey has a formidable military presence on the northern border of Iraq near the conflict that will emerge over the West's attempt to control the Middle East.

Beth-togarmah

The Hebrew word *beth* means "house," so Beth-togarmah means the "house of Togarmah." In Ezekiel 27:14, Togarmah is described as a nation that traded horses and mules with ancient Tyre. Ezekiel 38:6

states that the armies of Beth-togarmah will join in, too, from the distant north. Ancient Togarmah was also known as Til-garamu (Assyrian) or Tegarma (Hittite), and its territory is in modern Turkey, which is north of Israel. Again, Turkey is identified as part of this group of nations that attack Israel to challenge the Group of Ten.

Mapping the End Times

All the nations that will participate in the battle of Gog and Magog can be seen in the map below.

Based on these identifications, Ezekiel 38–39 predicts an invasion of the land of Israel in the last days by a vast confederation of nations from north of the Black and Caspian Seas, extending down to modern Iran in the east, as far as modern Libya to the west, and down to Sudan in the south. Therefore, Russia will have at least five key allies: Turkey, Iran, Libya, Sudan, and the Islamic nations of the former Soviet Union. Amazingly, all of these nations are Muslim nations, and Iran,

Battle of Gog and Magog

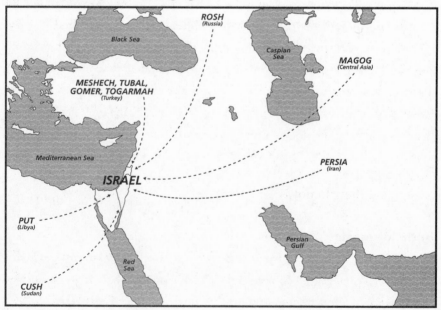

Libya, and Sudan are three of Israel's most ardent opponents. Many of these nations are hotbeds of militant Islam and are either forming or strengthening their ties with each other. This list of nations reads like the Who's Who of this week's newspaper. It does not require a very active imagination to envision these nations openly challenging the West and conspiring together to invade Israel in the near future.

THE PERIOD (EZEKIEL 38:8): WHEN?

One of the principal questions one could ask about this battle is: When is the battle going to occur? Clearly, it has not occurred in the past. But could it happen soon? What indications do we have in Ezekiel 38–39 about the timing of this invasion? Several opinions have been offered by capable Bible scholars on this point, and there has been considerable disagreement. Some have felt that the battle will take place before the Rapture; others believe it will take place in connection with the Battle of Armageddon at the end of the Great Tribulation. Some find it at the end of the Millennium, since there is a reference to Gog and Magog in Revelation 20:8.

It won't be possible to consider all these views in detail, but we're given some hints that suggest when this battle will take place. One of the clues given is that the battle will take place at a time when Israel has been regathered into its ancient land and is dwelling securely and at rest. There aren't too many times when Israel is at rest in God's prophetic program. The Jews have been scattered and persecuted over the face of the earth, and not even in the future will Israel have many periods of rest.

Certainly Israel is not at rest today. Israel is an armed camp, living under a truce with its Arab neighbors. Its enemies would drive every Israelite into the Mediterranean Sea and kill them if they could. The reason that they do not is because, humanly speaking, Israel has a good army that is more than a match for its neighbors. Today an armed truce and a no-man's-land separate Israel from its enemies.

Every young Israeli man is required to have three years of military training and every young woman two years of military training. While the women are trained for jobs that are not necessarily combatant, they also learn to use weapons, so that if they need to fight, they can. After military training, many of these young people are settled in villages near the border, where they can serve a double purpose—following their occupation, whatever it is, and serving as guards for the border of Israel. Israel's current state of unrest does not correspond to Ezekiel's prophecy. If Russia should invade the Middle East today, it would not be a fulfillment of this portion of Scripture. That has to take place when Israel is at rest.

One point at which Israel will be at rest is in the millennial kingdom. But we are told expressly that in the millennial kingdom there will be no war (Isaiah 2:4), and only when the rebellion occurs at the end of the Millennium when Satan is let loose (Revelation 20:7-9) does war break out. Certainly Israel is not going to be at rest under these circumstances either, once Satan is let loose.

Some have suggested that Israel will be at rest in the period of the Great Tribulation just before the second coming of Christ and that the prophecy of Russia will be fulfilled at that time. However, in the time of the Great Tribulation Israel will not be at rest, for Christ told them to flee to the mountains to escape their persecutors. Therefore the invasion described by Ezekiel could not be a part of the Battle of Armageddon at the end of the Great Tribulation.

There is only one period in the future that clearly fits this description of Ezekiel, and that is the first half of Daniel's seventieth week of God's program for Israel (Daniel 9:27). After the church has been raptured and saints have been raised from the dead and the living saints have been caught up to be with the Lord, a Group of Ten world leaders will lead a coalition of countries similar to the former Roman Empire. Out of the Group of Ten will come a strongman who will become its dictator (discussed in previous chapters). Daniel 9:26 states that "a ruler will arise." He will enter into a seven-year treaty of protection and peace with the people of Israel (Daniel 9:27).

Under that covenant, Israel will be able to relax, for their Gentile enemies will have become their friends, apparently guaranteeing their borders and promising them peace. Therefore, it seems clear that the battle will come when Israel has been lulled into the false security of the peace agreement signed by the leader of the revived Roman Empire. This peace treaty will be signed by the leader representing the combined economic and military power of the Western coalition. With these international guarantees, Israel will turn her energies toward increased wealth rather than defense—only to have the peace treaty shattered in less than four years.

Nevertheless, the first three and a half years of the Great Tribulation is the one time when a regathered Israel will be at rest and secure. Apparently Russia and her Islamic allies will invade the land of Israel during that period, possibly toward its close, and the Scripture will then be fulfilled.

THE PURPOSE (EZEKIEL 38:9-12): WHY?

The fourth key issue that is addressed in Ezekiel 38–39 is the purpose of this invasion. Both the human and the divine purpose for the invasion are given. The invading force will have four main goals:

1. Acquire more territory (38:8)
2. Amass wealth (38:12)
3. Destroy the people of Israel (38:11, 16)
4. Confront and challenge the Antichrist or the West who will be Israel's ally as a result of the treaty in Daniel 9:27. The divine purpose in allowing this invasion is expressed in Ezekiel 38:14-16. Through the attack God will be sanctified in the eyes of the nations.

THE PROCEEDINGS (EZEKIEL 38:13–39:20): WHAT?

Beginning in Ezekiel 38:13 and continuing through Ezekiel 39:20, the focus is on the fate of the invaders and the aftermath of the invasion. When these nations invade the land of Israel, it will look like the biggest mismatch in history. It will make the invasions of Israel in 1967 and

1973 by the Arab nations pale in comparison. When Russia assembles this last-days' strike force, it will look like Israel is finished. But God is in control of the entire situation. He will mount up in His fury to destroy these godless invaders. "But this is what the Sovereign LORD says: When Gog invades the land of Israel, my fury will boil over! In my jealousy and blazing anger, I promise a mighty shaking in the land of Israel on that day" (Ezekiel 38:18-19).

God will intervene to rescue His helpless people and will use four means to destroy Russia and her allies. The four means of destruction are listed in Ezekiel 38:19-22: a devastating earthquake; soldiers turning swords against each other; disease; and a cataclysmic combination of torrential rain, hailstones, fire, and burning sulphur. The famous Six Day War occurred in Israel in June 1967. This will be the "One Day War" or even the "One Hour War" when God supernaturally destroys this Russian-Islamic horde.

There are four key events that occur in the aftermath of this invasion:

1. **The Birds and the Beasts (Ezekiel 39:4-5, 17-20; Revelation 19:17-18).** The carnage that results from this slaughter will provide a great feast for the birds of the air and the beasts of the field. God refers to the carnage as "My sacrificial feast" and "My banquet table," to which He invites the birds and the beasts as His guests.

2. **The Burying of the Dead for Seven Months (Ezekiel 39:11-12, 14-16).** Clean-up squads will be assembled to go through the land. They will set up markers wherever they see a human bone. When the gravediggers come behind them they will see the markers and take the remains to the Valley of Gog's Hordes for burial. The cleansing will be so extensive that a town will be established in the valley at the gravesites to aid those who are cleansing the land. The name of the town will be Hamonah (horde).

3. The Burning of the Weapons for Seven Years (Ezekiel 39:9-10).

The burning of weapons (spears, bows, and arrows) for seven years has led some to wonder if the nations will regress to using primitive weapons in the end times. Others maintain that Ezekiel used ancient weapons that were familiar in his day to describe and anticipate modern weapons. We are not in a position today to settle this problem with any finality. Whatever the explanation, the most sensible interpretation is that the passage refers to actual weapons pressed into use because of the peculiar circumstances of that day.

Because Ezekiel 39:9 mentions the weapons will be burned for seven years, many place this invasion before the seven-year tribulation period. Yet as has been mentioned, Ezekiel 38 makes it clear that Israel will be at peace when this invasion occurs, and it is difficult to picture Israel living peacefully before the Rapture. Of course, this means the burning of weapons will continue for the first few years of the millennial reign of Christ after His second coming. This will be part of the ongoing cleansing of the land after Christ establishes His Kingdom on earth.

4. The Blessing of Salvation (Ezekiel 39:22).

In the midst of His wrath and fury, God will also pour out His grace and mercy (39:22). God will use the awesome display of His power against Russia and her allies to bring many—both Jews and Gentiles—to salvation. Many of those who turn to the true God as a result of this demonstration of His power will undoubtedly be among the vast group of the redeemed in Revelation 7:9-14.

THE PROPHETIC SIGNIFICANCE: HOW?

The final question to consider is how the world stage today is being set for the fulfillment of this incredible prophecy. What are some of the key developments we are witnessing today that point toward this invasion? What recent or current developments correspond with

Ezekiel's prophecy? There are eight major events in the last sixty years that point toward the fulfillment of Ezekiel's prophecy.

Israel Will Be Regathered

First, for the events of Ezekiel 38–39 to be fulfilled Israel must be regathered to her land in unbelief. Ezekiel 38 follows the famous dry bones vision in Ezekiel 37 that pictures the physical restoration of Judah and Israel to the land followed by her spiritual restoration to the Lord. In Ezekiel 37 the restoration occurs in stages. It begins with restoration to the land in unbelief. Unbelieving Israel's initial regathering is further confirmed by the fact that only after the battle of Gog and Magog do many in Israel turn to the Lord (Ezekiel 39:22).

As we saw in chapter 4, Israel's regathering in unbelief has occurred dramatically in stages beginning in 1871 and continuing up to the present day. Thus, what we see happening before our eyes, the restored unbelieving Jewish state, is a necessary precondition for Ezekiel's prophecy to be fulfilled.

Israel Must Possess the Mountains of Israel

Second, according to Ezekiel 39:2-4, Israel must possess the "mountains of Israel" when this invasion occurs. God tells the future invaders: "I will turn you around and drive you toward the mountains of Israel, bringing you from the distant north. I will knock the bow from your left hand and the arrows from your right hand, and I will leave you helpless. You and your army and your allies will all die on the mountains. I will feed you to the vultures and wild animals." The famous Six Day War in Israel in 1967 helped set the stage for this to be fulfilled. Before the Six Day War all of the mountains of Israel, with the exception of a small strip of West Jerusalem, were entirely in the hands of the Jordanian Arabs. Only since 1967 have the mountains *of* Israel been *in* Israel, thus setting the stage for the fulfillment of this prophecy.

Israel Must Be at Peace

Third, according to Ezekiel 38, Israel must be "at rest" and "living securely" when this invasion occurs. The drive for peace in the Middle East has consumed Western diplomats and dominated world news. From the Oslo Accords to the Road Map for Peace, brokering a peace agreement between Israel and her neighbors is one of the major international priorities. A peaceful solution to the Israeli-Palestinian crisis is integrally linked to stability in the Middle East and Persian Gulf. The ongoing quest for Middle East peace points toward the peace treaty in Daniel 9:27 and the period of security in Ezekiel 38.

Russia Reclaims Its Lost Glory

Fourth, one of the most significant international developments in the last fifty years, one that is a necessary prerequisite for this invasion, is the remarkable rise of Russia to a place of world prominence. Along with the United States, Russia (previously the Soviet Union) has been one of the world's great military powers. Although some hopeful signs of democracy appeared in Russia after the dissolution of the Soviet Union in 1991, there are growing fears that Russia today is regressing back to her old totalitarian, autocratic ways. Russian president Vladimir Putin and many of the key leaders in his government served as officers in the KGB. Putin has made numerous moves to centralize authority. Experts maintain that Russia's oil wealth is allowing Putin to take the country back toward autocracy without any public outcry.[9]

Russia has a vital interest in the Middle East and Persian Gulf. This is her neighborhood. Some control over this area is vital to Russia's national security. Moreover, since the fall of the Soviet empire, the great Russian bear has been like a mother bear robbed of her cubs. The fall of her empire brought national humiliation. In April 2005, during his annual state of the nation address, Putin declared that the collapse of the Soviet Union was "the greatest geopolitical catastrophe" of the century.[10] He seems to long for the good old days of the U.S.S.R. For Russia, an invasion of Israel with an Islamic coalition would be an opportunity for her to reclaim her lost glory and assert control over the Middle East.

Ezekiel 38:1-5 lists "Rosh" (Russia) and "Persia" (Iran) as allies against Israel in the end times. This prophecy was written almost 2,600 years ago and yet reads like today's headlines. The Russian-Iranian alliance is becoming cozier all the time. Here are just a couple of troubling examples of this emerging partnership: Russia sold Iran a nuclear reactor and later sold twenty-nine of its most advanced missile systems to the radical regime for a pricey one billion dollars. These missiles would be used against U.S. or Israeli planes should they attempt to take out Iran's nuclear facilities. Furthermore, Russia consistently obstructs any meaningful U.N. sanctions against Iran for its nuclear program.

Hatred of Israel Will Increase

Fifth, the rise of pandemic Islamic fundamentalism with its virulent anti-Semitism and hatred of the restored Jewish state provides a powerful motivation for this invasion. While Islam is and always has been a religion of violence and terror, the modern rise of the Islamic terrorist state began in early 1979 in Iran when the Shah was ousted by the Ayatollah Khomeini. Iran has exported this terror movement to neighboring Islamic nations. Of course, Ezekiel does not mention Islam or terrorism as a driving force behind this invasion since Islam did not exist until the seventh century AD. However, today all the geographical areas other than Russia that he identified as participants in this invasion are identifiable Islamic nations (Central Asia, Libya, Sudan, Iran, and Turkey). This sets the stage for the final jihad into Israel depicted in Ezekiel's prophecy. For these Islamic allies the Gog and Magog invasion will be an opening to drive Israel into the sea and lure the West into a final clash of civilizations since Israel will be protected by her covenant with the Antichrist.

Iran Becomes a Key Player

Sixth, Iran (Persia) is a key player on the world scene today as required by Ezekiel 38:5. Clearly, Iran is public enemy number one today in the

West and in Israel. As home to radical jihadists and a supporter of terror groups around the world, Iran cannot be allowed to possess nuclear weapons. This is unthinkable. Therefore, we can expect a great deal of focus on Iran in the near future. And all of this is greatly exacerbated and complicated by the fact that Iran has about 10 percent of the world's proven oil reserves. Uncertainty over the situation in Iran is part of the reason that oil prices neared an all-time high during the week of August 8–12, 2005, closing at over sixty-five dollars a barrel.

To make matters even worse, in June 2005 the Iranian people elected the hard-liner Mahmoud Ahmadinejad as their new president.[11] He is the former mayor of Tehran and a former Revolutionary Guard commander. On October 26, 2005, he said flat out that Israel should be "wiped off the map" and that "anyone who signs a treaty which [recognizes] the entity of Israel means he has signed the surrender of the Muslim world." He further called for Iranians "to riot against Zionists [Israel] and unbelievers" in a nationwide demonstration on Friday, October 28, 2005, during al-Quds—or Jerusalem—Day. Ahmadinejad participated in the large demonstration himself along with others who backed his call for the destruction of the Jewish state. The marchers carried placards that read, "Death to Israel, death to America." Iran's new president has also stated that the Holocaust never occurred and that the Jewish state should be relocated to Europe. All of this inflammatory rhetoric comes at a time when the United Nations is cautiously dealing with Iran about sanctions over its resumption of its nuclear program. Needless to say, tensions in the region are mounting. Iran is awash in oil money and is earnestly seeking nuclear weapons.

On January 9, 2006, Iran broke the seals that International Atomic Energy Agency (IAEA) inspectors had placed on two nuclear plants, the Uranium Conversion Facility in Isfahan and the centrifuge plant at Natanz. Iran then restarted its nuclear program, breaking a two-and-a-half-year moratorium.[12]

On April 11, 2006, another key milestone in the Iran crisis was reached. At that time Ahmadinejad made several announcements:

I am officially announcing that Iran has joined the group of countries which have nuclear technology.

At this historical juncture, I announce, in shadow of the Mahdi, the lord of time—may we hasten his return—through the sacrifices of our scientists and our devoted youth and the prayers of our brave people, we have mastered the nuclear fuel cycle on a laboratory scale. And we have enriched uranium to the necessary level for nuclear power generation.

I formally declare that Iran has joined the club of nuclear countries.[13]

Ahmadinejad has made a number of anti-Semitic statements:

No doubt the new wave [of attacks] in Palestine will soon wipe off this disgraceful blot [Israel] from the face of the Islamic world.[14]

Israel must be wiped off the map. . . . The establishment of a Zionist regime was a move by the world oppressor against the Islamic world. . . . The skirmishes in the occupied land are part of the war of destiny. The outcome of hundreds of years of war will be defined in Palestinian land.

Although the main solution is for the elimination of the Zionist regime, at this stage an immediate cease-fire must be implemented.

A new Middle East will prevail without the existence of Israel.

Are they human beings? . . . They [Zionists] are a group of bloodthirsty savages putting all other criminals to shame.

Israel is destined for destruction and will soon disappear . . . a contradiction to nature, we foresee its rapid disappearance and destruction.

The Zionists and their protectors are the most detested people in all of humanity, and the hatred is increasing every day.

The occupying regime of Palestine has actually pushed the button of its own destruction by launching a new round of invasion and barbaric onslaught on Lebanon.[15]

At a meeting in April 2006, he made more inflammatory comments. He said that Palestine "will soon be freed." He referred to Israel as a "constant threat" and "permanent threat to the Middle East" and said the Middle East will "soon be liberated." In one of his most revealing statements, the Iranian president said, "The Zionist regime is an injustice and by its very nature a permanent threat. Whether you like it or not, the Zionist regime is heading toward annihilation. The Zionist regime is a rotten, dried tree that will be eliminated by one storm."[16] Could this be a threat of a nuclear attack against Israel? What could annihilate Israel by one storm other than a nuclear bomb?

Ahmadinejad's government, along with Syria, is the primary supporter of Hezbollah and Hamas. In late 2006, Iran pledged $120 million to the Hamas-led Palestinian government.[17] This "aid" will certainly be used to buy weapons and prepare for an attack against Israel.

Ahmadinejad's fanatical hatred of Israel is permeating the news media in Iran. An editorial titled "Preparations for the Great War" appeared in *Resalat*, one of Iran's daily newspapers. The editorial said, "The great war is ahead of us, [and will break out] perhaps tomorrow, or in another few days, or in a few months, or even in a few years. For the first time in the 60 years of its disgraceful life, the Zionist regime—the West's beloved in the Middle East—tasted the taste of defeat, and the citizens of this regime trembled at the menace of Hizbullah's missiles. . . . The nation of Muslims must prepare for the great war, so as to completely wipe out the Zionist regime, and remove this cancerous growth. Like the Imam (Ayatollah) Khomeini said: 'Israel must collapse.'"[18]

Another conservative Iranian newspaper, *Keyhan,* printed this bellicose statement, "Hizbullah destroyed at least half of Israel in the Lebanon war. . . . Now only half the path (to its destruction) remains.

. . . Just as in one 33-day [sic] war more than 50 percent of Israel was destroyed, and the hope of its supporters for the continued life of this regime was broken, it is likely that in the next battle, the second half will also collapse."[19]

Ahmadinejad and the Apocalypse

Not only does Ahmadinejad make provocative statements, but he is motivated by an end-of-days messianism that feeds his warped sense of divine destiny. He believes the apocalypse will occur in his own lifetime, and his statements suggest that he believes his destiny is to bring about the end times and usher in the coming of the Islamic messiah.

As a Shiite Muslim, Iran's president is deeply committed to an Islamic messianic figure known as the Mahdi (Arabic for "rightly guided one"), sometimes referred to as the Hidden Imam (leader). He seeks to bring apocalypse upon the world and is fixated on what is known in Islam as Mahdaviat—quite simply, this is the desire to help prepare for the Mahdi.

Ahmadinejad appears to believes he is invincible. He declares, "I have a connection with God, since God said infidels will have no way to harm believers. . . . We have [only] one step before we attain the summit of nuclear technology. . . . The West will not dare to attack us."[20]

Reporter Anton La Guardia, writing for the online British news source telegraph.co.uk, points out that all Muslims expect a divine savior, the Mahdi, to appear in the earth's final days. Ahmadinejad and his cabinet are rumored to have signed a contract pledging to work for his return. La Guardia says Muslims believe that the Mahdi's "return will be preceded by cosmic chaos, war and bloodshed. After a cataclysmic confrontation with evil and darkness, the Mahdi will lead the world to an era of universal peace."

He adds, "Mr. Ahmadinejad appears to believe that these events are close at hand and that ordinary mortals can influence the divine time-table. The prospect of such a man obtaining nuclear weapons is worrying. The unspoken question is this: is Mr. Ahmadinejad now tempting a

Islamic Beliefs about the Mahdi

1. Islam's primary awaited savior
2. Descendant of Muhammad
3. Caliph and Imam of Muslims worldwide
4. Unparalleled political, military, and religious world leader
5. Revealed after a period of great turmoil and suffering on earth
6. Establishes justice throughout the world
7. Leads a revolution to establish a new world order
8. Will go to war against all nations who oppose him
9. Makes a seven-year peace treaty with a Jew of priestly lineage
10. Conquers Israel for Islam and leads final battle against the Jews
11. Rules for seven years in Jerusalem
12. Causes Islam to be the only religion on earth
13. Discovers biblical manuscripts that convince Jews to convert
14. Brings the Ark of the Covenant from the Sea of Galilee to Jerusalem
15. Has the power from Allah over wind, rain, and crops
16. Will possess and distribute great wealth
17. Face will shine like a star and will be loved by all

* Randall Price, "The 'Second Coming' of Islam," *World of the Bible News and Views* 8, no.1 (Summer 2006): 3. Used with permission.

clash with the West because he feels safe in the belief of the imminent return of the Hidden Imam? Worse, might he be trying to provoke chaos in the hope of hastening his reappearance?"[21]

Iran is dominated by Shiite Islam, whose spiritual leaders, called Imams, are bloodline relatives of the prophet Ali, Muhammad's cousin. There is a prophecy in Islam about the coming of the Twelfth Imam— Muhammad al-Mahdi. The Twelver sect believes he was born in AD 868 and disappeared in AD 874 into the cave of the great mosque of Samarra (in modern Iraq) without leaving any descendants. They teach that the Twelfth Imam was still active and communicated by messengers until AD 941 when all communication and contact with this world was cut off.[22]

According to Islamic teaching, he will return near the end of the world to rule the earth for seven years and bring about the final judgment and end of the world.[23] This seven-year rule for the Mahdi is interesting because the Bible predicts that the Antichrist or false messiah will dominate the earth for seven years, ruling the entire world for the final half of the seven-year period. It's possible that the Islamic expectation of a messiah who will rule for seven years could set them up to initially accept such a leader who will make a seven-year peace treaty according to Daniel 9:27.

Ahmadinejad's view of the end times is also influenced by his close ties with the messianic Hojatieh society, led by Ayatollah Mesbah Yazdi. Twelvers believe that until the Twelfth Imam returns, every true Muslim must put himself under the authority of a holy man known as an ayatollah, who is able to mediate salvation. This spiritual leader often appears with the new president in public. The Hojatieh believe that only great tribulation, increased violence, and conflict will bring about his coming. The "creation of chaos on earth," they believe, can speed up the Imam's return. For Ahmadinejad, an all-out war with the West would be an open invitation for the return of the Mahdi.[24]

The president's apocalyptic view is so strongly ingrained that he fired Iran's most experienced diplomats and many other officials who don't share his view of the coming apocalyptic conflict, replacing them with fellow zealots.[25] On November 16, 2005, in a speech in Tehran to senior clerics, Ahmadinejad said that the primary mission of his regime was to "pave the path for the glorious reappearance of the Imam Mahdi (May God Hasten His Reappearance)."[26]

Ahmadinejad gave a speech at the United Nations in September 2005 that many were expecting to be diplomatic. But they were shocked when he spoke in apocalyptic terms and ended the speech with a messianic appeal to God to "hasten the emergence of your last repository, the Promised One, that perfect and pure human being, the one that will fill this world with justice and peace."

Ahmadinejad provided his own account of the U.N. address and his otherworldly experience:

> One of our group told me that when I started to say "In the name of God the almighty and merciful," he saw a light around me, and I was placed inside this aura. I felt it myself. I felt the atmosphere suddenly change, and for those 27 or 28 minutes, the leaders of the world did not blink. . . . And they were rapt. It seemed as if a hand was holding them there and had opened their eyes to receive the message from the Islamic republic.[27]

This account is reminiscent of Hitler's mesmerizing, satanic speeches to the German people. German chancellor Angela Merkel has openly compared the Iranian president to Adolf Hitler. Yet reporter Anton La Guardia offers a different interpretation of the reason for the audience's reaction:

> Western officials said the real reason for any open-eyed stares from delegates was that "they couldn't believe what they were hearing from Ahmadinejad." Their sneaking suspicion is that he relishes a clash with the West in the conviction that it would rekindle the spirit of the Islamic revolution and speed up the arrival of the Hidden Imam.[28]

Mortimer Zuckerman warns the West to be aware of the Iranian president's real intentions: "His foreign policy ambition is an Islamic government for the whole world, under the leadership of the Mahdi, the absent Imam of the Shiites—code language for the export of radical Islam. And he casts himself as Hitler reincarnated, calling for Israel to be 'wiped off the map.' Who can think that Iran poses no threat to world peace? History tells us that when madmen call for genocide, they usually mean it."[29]

Turkey Aligns with Islamic Neighbors

The seventh event necessary before the battle of Gog and Magog occurs is this: Turkey must be willing to join the coalition of nations against Israel. For years, this seemed highly unlikely, since Turkey has made every attempt to become part of the European Union. With great fanfare on October 3, 2005, the European Union launched formal negotiations in Brussels to discuss Turkey's admittance to membership in the European club. Several months earlier European leaders had decided to open talks to consider Turkey's admission to the EU. Even the possibility of this merger was hailed as the meeting of East and West.

However, it now appears certain that the EU will reject Turkey's bid for admission. Both France and the Netherlands rejected the proposed EU constitution, and one of their main objections was the notion of enlargement, especially admitting Turkey to the EU. Support for Turkish accession among the fifteen EU countries that have been members the longest is only at 32 percent. However, the EU does not want to alienate the Turks; thus, the EU appears to be stringing Turkey along for geopolitics. There are five key reasons the EU will reject Turkey:

1. *It is a Muslim country.* Islam phobia is on the rise in Europe. This feeling will be heightened in light of terrorist attacks on European soil.
2. *It is too big.* With 70 million people, Turkey would be the second largest EU nation, behind Germany.
3. *It is agrarian.* The EU supports farmers with huge subsidies.
4. *It is poor.* Turkey's gross domestic product per capita is only 27 percent of the national average.
5. *It has enemies.* Turkey faces two historic enemies within the EU: Greece and Cyprus.[30]

These developments are interesting, because the Bible predicts in Ezekiel 38 that Turkey will be part of a massive Russian-led invasion of Israel in the end times. The main countries that will participate in this invasion are Russia, Iran, Libya, Sudan, Central Asian nations, and Turkey. At present the government of Vladimir Putin in Russia is gaining greater control and appears to be moving back toward the days of communist dictatorship. Iran, Libya, Sudan, and the nations of Central Asia are all predominantly Islamic, and it is not too difficult to see them all joining in for one last jihad against Israel. As Turkey moved more and more toward the West, it appeared highly unlikely that she would ally herself with a Russian-Islamic coalition against Israel. But that seems to be changing. Turkey's admission to the EU now seems hopeless. And when Turkey is rejected by the West, she will have to look elsewhere to bolster her strategic ambitions.

The AKP (Justice and Development party) of Prime Minister Recep Tayyip Erdogan is an avowedly secular party, but with Islamic roots. It poses a difficult challenge to Turkey's eighty-year-old secularism, founded by Mustafa Ataturk. It seems clear that the AKP wants to move the country and its foreign policy in a more Islamic direction. In recent months, Erdogan has reached out to some very unsavory characters in Turkey's neighborhood. He visited President Bashar Assad of Syria in early 2005 and traveled to Iran to meet with the Iranian mullahs.

Erdogan's chief adviser, Ahmet Davutoglu, is the driving force behind Turkey's foreign policy changes. He is now contending that Turkey has an historic opportunity to be a leader in the Muslim world. He also believes that her geographic position requires improved relations with Russia. Earlier this year, overcoming decades of enmity, Turkey signed a trade pact with Russia. At the same time Turkey is being rebuffed by Europe and is warming relations with Russia, anti-Semitism in Turkey has been growing. According to a recent article, "At any bookstore in Istanbul or Ankara you will find prominently displayed Adolph Hitler's *Mein Kampf*, a popular seller these days."[31]

While there may be many twists and turns in Turkey and other nations of the world before the Rapture occurs, what is occurring right now appears to be moving Turkey back toward Russia and the Muslim world just as one would expect if the battle of Gog and Magog is near.

Saudi Arabia Aligns with the West

Eighth, Ezekiel 38:13 (NASB) mentions "Sheba and Dedan and the merchants of Tarshish" as lodging a lame protest against the Gog and Magog invasion of Israel. There is general agreement that Sheba and Dedan inhabited northern Arabia, or what today is Saudi Arabia.

Ezekiel 38:13 indicates that Saudi Arabia and its Western allies will object to this invasion by Russia and an Islamic horde. Although Saudi Arabia is no great friend of the West, she is the one Islamic nation that consistently serves her own self-interest by conveniently allying herself with Western nations. Thus, the mention of a protest by Sheba, Dedan, and Tarshish corresponds with current developments.

Events in our world today indicate that the great Battle of Gog and Magog in Ezekiel 38–39 could be very near. All of the necessary antecedents for the fulfillment of this prophecy are in place or are moving in that direction. The Jewish people have been regathered to their land in unbelief, the Middle East peace process is front and center in international diplomacy, and the invaders in Ezekiel 38 are identifiable nations who have both the desire and the potential to fulfill the Gog prophecy.

The remarkable correspondence between world events and what Ezekiel predicted is another indication that the coming of the Lord could be very soon.

RUSSIA'S LOSS—THE ANTICHRIST'S GAIN

As will be discussed in the next chapter, Russia's attack on Israel will not simply be an attack on Israel alone, but it will be a challenge to the peace and protection promised by the new leader of the Western coalition. By this time the emergence of the powerful new alignment of Europe and the Middle East will have seriously limited Russia's role in the world. The attack by Russia will be a desperate attempt to recoup her position as a world power with influence over the Middle East.

The attack on Israel will transpire as a direct confrontation between

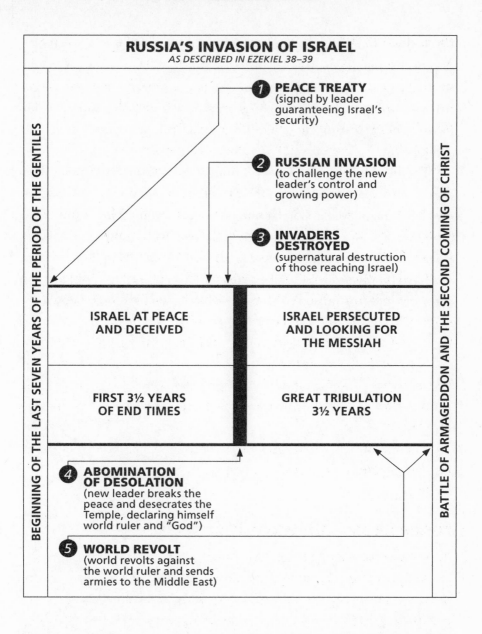

RUSSIA'S INVASION OF ISRAEL
AS DESCRIBED IN EZEKIEL 38–39

1 PEACE TREATY
(signed by leader guaranteeing Israel's security)

2 RUSSIAN INVASION
(to challenge the new leader's control and growing power)

3 INVADERS DESTROYED
(supernatural destruction of those reaching Israel)

BEGINNING OF THE LAST SEVEN YEARS OF THE PERIOD OF THE GENTILES

BATTLE OF ARMAGEDDON AND THE SECOND COMING OF CHRIST

ISRAEL AT PEACE AND DECEIVED

ISRAEL PERSECUTED AND LOOKING FOR THE MESSIAH

FIRST 3½ YEARS OF END TIMES

GREAT TRIBULATION 3½ YEARS

4 ABOMINATION OF DESOLATION
(new leader breaks the peace and desecrates the Temple, declaring himself world ruler and "God")

5 WORLD REVOLT
(world revolts against the world ruler and sends armies to the Middle East)

Russia and her Islamic allies and the new leader of the Western coalition. With the United States in isolation, the balance of power in the world will have shifted so that the revived Roman Empire is on one side and Russia and her allies are on the other. Because of this, the destruction of the Russian army becomes tremendously significant.

Once this occurs during the Battle of Gog and Magog, the balance of power will fall dramatically into the hands of the new world leader that emerges from the Group of Ten. This greatly changed world situation will position him as the most powerful and charismatic ruler in the world, setting the stage for the apocalyptic events that will soon follow.

The threat of Russian intervention in the Middle East is real. Her current financial diplomacy in the Middle East will not be sufficient to give her a major role in determining the area's future. Her eventual bid for power will be a military disaster. In the end, Russia and her unwitting allies will reap a terrible judgment from God for their blasphemy, terror, and hostility toward Israel. Like many nations before, they will feel the curse of God—promised to all those who curse His chosen people.

 See how today's headlines relate to this chapter at http://www.prophecyhotline.com.

CHAPTER 8

THE COMING WORLD DICTATOR: "THE WORLD IS MINE, AND I AM GOD"

EVENT #7: One leader seizes power by uniting the military and economic powers of the West— declaring himself world ruler.

When the Jews return to Zion, and
A comet rips the sky,
And the Holy Roman Empire rises
Then you and I must die.

From the eternal sea he rises,
Creating armies on either shore;
Turning man against his brother
'Till man exists no more.

THE OMEN (1 9 7 6)

IN THE HISTORY OF THE world many a great man has dreamed of someday having the world at his feet. In the Middle East many great nations have risen and fallen. Egypt was a powerful nation in the Middle East fifteen hundred years before Christ—followed by Assyria with her capital at Nineveh. Nebuchadnezzar, the great king of Babylon, carved out an expansive empire that included most of western Asia.

About three hundred years before Christ, Alexander the Great and his armies swept as far east as India and for a brief time ruled all of western Asia, northern Africa, and southeast Europe. At the time of Christ the Roman Caesars had subdued southern Europe, northern Africa, and western Asia to form the greatest empire ever known in history. In more modern times, Napoleon dreamed of world conquest only to have his dreams shattered at Waterloo. In the twentieth century Hitler dreamed of someday having the world at his feet.

But none of these men ever really conquered the entire world. The military conquerors of the ancient world at best conquered portions of Europe, North Africa, and western Asia, but no world ruler has ever controlled all of the three major continents related to the Middle East, much less the nations of the Western Hemisphere: North America, Central America, and South America. Until our generation, a universal world government wasn't really possible.

The advances of modern technology in communication, transportation, and the weapons of war have suddenly shrunk our world. A missile can reach any part of the world in less than thirty minutes. Television, radio, and the Internet provide instant communication. A world where men could once live in relative isolation is now geographically one. Every major event, whether it is an oil embargo, the development of a new nuclear weapon, or the threat of starvation, is now covered by international television that brings distant events into the homes of people around the world. Men and nations can no longer live in isolation.

During and following World War I, for the first time, steps were taken to form an international body to prevent further world wars. The resulting League of Nations, however, was unsuccessful. With Congress already disillusioned by the practical results of World War I, the United States was not ready for such a role in world affairs. The idea of world government seemed unnecessary for a country oceans away from problems in Europe and Asia. But the earth was growing smaller, and America's isolation could not last for long. In 1941, the United States once again was drawn into a world war. The attack on Pearl Harbor marked the end of America's attempt to ignore her responsibilities in a shrinking world.

By the end of World War II, a frightening new dimension had been added to the need for a world government. Although the war itself was devastating and extended throughout more of the world than any previous war had, it ended with the atomic holocaust of Hiroshima and Nagasaki, Japan. With the advent of the atomic bomb, no nation or people would ever be safe again. The destructive capabilities of war had increased to a degree never before considered possible.

Nuclear destruction threatened not only military forces but entire cities and civilian populations. Now a war of days or weeks could destroy the entire world. The time had come for a new international world organization.

WORLD GOVERNMENT—MAN'S LAST HOPE

A shared global fear of a major conflict involving atomic weaponry gave birth to the United Nations in 1946. Though it included only a portion of the world's nations at first, the United Nations soon grew to include most of them. With the admission of China, all the major nations and most of the smaller nations became part of this international structure. But the United Nations lacked the power and authority to prevent war. Throughout history, its weakness has been demonstrated again and again. Its failure to solve the conflict in Southeast Asia and its continued inability to prevent conflict in the Middle East has demonstrated that the United Nations is not the final answer.

Still, some form of universal government seems the only hope for a world that could easily destroy itself. The problems facing the world—terrorism, nuclear war, overpopulation, starvation, pollution, and economic instability—are international problems. Even terrorist groups like Al-Qaeda and Hezbollah now threaten the delicate web of international interdependence. New economic challenges face the world. There simply will not be enough oil to fuel the economies of the West, India, and China. The international distribution of resources and the control of currencies will soon necessitate regulation by some type of world agency. The United Nations, the Common Market, and the World Bank are only the beginning of a quest for some solution to the world's increasing problems.

Many international leaders and intellectuals believe that a strong and effective world government is the only hope for the survival of man on this planet. For instance, at the United Nations in December 1988, Mikhail Gorbachev said, "Further global progress is now possible only through a quest for universal consensus in the movement towards a new world order."[1] As these attitudes are increasingly expressed in our time, it is important to ask what the Bible says on this subject. As a matter of fact, the prophets anticipated just such a state of affairs in the world as the end times approach.

DANIEL'S PROPHECY OF WORLD EMPIRES

The prophets may never have realized the modern reasons for a world government, but they did predict that history would end in one central government that would attempt to encompass the entire world. The Bible not only predicted the rise and fall of history's strongest world empires, but with prophetic accuracy has described the events that will lead to a final world government before the second coming of Christ.

As we have already seen in chapter 6, the prophet Daniel, for instance, described the series of developments that will bring the entire earth to a final world government, which will reach its climax when Christ returns to judge the nations and set up His Kingdom on earth (Daniel 7). Daniel predicted with accuracy the progression of preceding world empires. The first empire described by Daniel was that of Babylon, which conquered Jerusalem when Daniel was a teenager. As a prophet during the Babylonian exile, Daniel predicted the fall of the Babylonian empire and the rise of the Medes and the Persians, which he witnessed during his lifetime. But most important, Daniel revealed a prophetic list of all the world empires that would rise and fall before the second coming of Christ. Daniel's prophecy offers a complete outline of the history of world empires written before these empires existed. This outline is so essential to the understanding of the future of the nations that Jesus related His predictions to events in Daniel's prophecy.

Daniel's outline of world empires included the empire of Greece and the Roman Empire. Daniel also anticipated a final stage to the Roman Empire that has not yet come to fruition. It is this final world empire and its world dictator that will push the world toward Armageddon. In that final clash of nations, the history of empires built by conquest will be ended forever by the second coming of Christ. Empires and governments created by men will be replaced by the direct rule of God on earth—a final millennium of peace, righteousness, and prosperity before history ends in a new heaven and a new earth.

Daniel named the empires of Babylon, the Medes and the Persians, and of Alexander the Great in his prophecies. After the decline and fall of the Greek city-states, the next empire to arise was that of Rome, which came into power in the centuries preceding the coming of Christ. This fourth empire was not named by Daniel but was described as "terrifying, dreadful, and very strong. It devoured and crushed its victims with huge iron teeth and trampled their remains beneath its feet. It was different from any of the other beasts, and it had ten horns" (Daniel 7:7). The armies of Rome crushed all opposition and extended the iron control of the Caesars over all of southern Europe, western Asia, and North Africa. But Daniel also observed that in the last stage of the empire the iron would be mixed with baked clay, implying that the fourth kingdom would be vulnerable to sudden destruction, just as pottery can easily be shattered (Daniel 2:41-45).

According to Daniel's prophecy, this fourth empire of the Caesars, although seemingly destroyed, is not actually dead and gone. A final form of the last empire is destined to emerge when ten leaders from nations originally in the Roman Empire emerge from a new union of Europe and Mediterranean nations (Daniel 7:7).

Daniel's vision of this stage of the Roman Empire involves a beast, symbolically representing the Roman Empire, with the ten horns on the beast representing ten kings yet to rise on the stage of world history. The interpretation of the prophecy was directly given to Daniel, as recorded in Daniel 7:23-24: "This fourth beast is the fourth world power that will rule the earth. It will be different from all the others. It will devour the whole world, trampling and crushing everything in its path. Its ten horns are ten kings who will rule that empire."

The first phase of Rome's rise to power and the empire's division and decline are now ancient history. But the final phase of the fourth kingdom has not yet occurred. This has led students of biblical prophecy to expect a new concentration of power to emerge in Europe and the Mediterranean. The fourth world empire will be revived as a final prelude to Armageddon and the second coming of Christ.

The first movements toward the revival of the fourth empire are in today's headlines as Europe moves toward the revival of the Roman Empire. This will set the stage for the emergence of the new world dictator.

THE COMING DICTATOR'S FIRST MOVE

A new world dictator will first reveal himself in the role of a peace-maker in the Middle East. This event will take place during the first stage of the revived Roman Empire, the fourth world empire described by Daniel. Symbolically the new world leader is depicted as "another small horn" who will emerge from the ten-leader oligarchy controlling the political and military power of the West (Daniel 7:8). Daniel described his vision of the new world ruler's rise to power in these words: "As I was looking at the horns, suddenly another small horn appeared among them. Three of the first horns were torn out by the roots to make room for it. This little horn had eyes like human eyes and a mouth that was boasting arrogantly" (Daniel 7:8).

The Group of Ten that consolidates the power and wealth of the Middle East will soon come under the control of this new leader. Bible expositors have concluded that this emerging ruler will first of all subdue three of the original ten leaders and then take control of the entire coalition. The leaders will yield control of the new European Union to this new strong man of the hour.

Daniel identified this man as the one who eventually will become the final world dictator, the Antichrist described in Revelation. He is described as different from the other ten leaders, speaking out against God, persecuting believers in God, and growing in power until he controls the entire world for a period of forty-two months.

The interpretation given to Daniel is, "Then another king will arise, different from the other ten, who will subdue three of them. He will defy the Most High and oppress the holy people of the Most High. He will try to change their sacred festivals and laws, and they will be placed under his control for a time, times, and half a time" (Daniel 7:24-25).

The time period of his absolute rule can be calculated as a year, plus two years, plus half a year—three and a half years (Daniel 12:11; Revelation 13:5).

UNDERSTANDING DANIEL'S SEVENTY WEEKS

Daniel's prophecy provides the key to the entire drama of the last days. The new world leader will cause a series of world-shattering events, which are described in detail by Daniel and the writer of the book of Revelation. Jesus identified this man as the final military conqueror who will invade Jerusalem and desecrate the Temple, "'the abomination that causes desolation,' spoken of through the prophet Daniel" (Matthew 24:15, NIV).

In Daniel 9:24-27 the prophet recorded a revelation of seventy "sevens" of years, which totals 490 years, in which great events would take place in relation to Jerusalem and the Jewish people. The first two major time segments involved 483 years, or sixty-nine "sevens." The word translated *week* (KJV) actually means "seven" and refers to years, not days. We know that this refers to years for two main reasons.

Daniel's Seventy Weeks

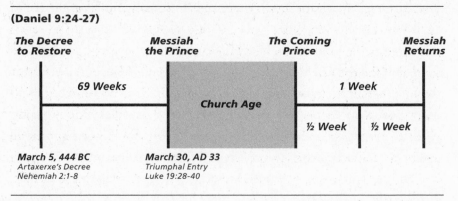

(Daniel 9:24-27)

| The Decree to Restore | Messiah the Prince | The Coming Prince | Messiah Returns |

69 Weeks | Church Age | 1 Week

½ Week | ½ Week

March 5, 444 BC
Artaxerxe's Decree
Nehemiah 2:1-8

March 30, AD 33
Triumphal Entry
Luke 19:28-40

First, nothing of any significance happened within a 490-day period after Daniel's prophecy. Second, according to Daniel 9:2, Daniel was already thinking in terms of years in the same context. This period was described by Daniel in these words: "Know and understand this: From the issuing of the decree to restore and rebuild Jerusalem until the Anointed One, the ruler, comes, there will be seven 'sevens,' and sixty-two 'sevens.' It will be rebuilt with streets and a trench, but in times of trouble. After the sixty-two 'sevens,' the Anointed One will be cut off and will have nothing. The people of the ruler who will come will destroy the city and the sanctuary. The end will come like a flood: War will continue until the end, and desolations have been decreed" (Daniel 9:25-26, NIV).

The first time segment of Daniel's seventy weeks began with the decree to restore and rebuild Jerusalem, the decree given to Nehemiah on March 5, 444 BC. The first seven weeks, or forty-nine years, marked the time needed to rebuild Jerusalem. The second segment of sixty-two weeks of years (434 years) marked the time that would pass until the Messiah was cut off. Adding these two segments reveals the amazing accuracy of Daniel's prophecy; the 483 years ended on March 30, AD 33, just before Jesus was rejected by the nation of Israel and crucified.[2]

But one week of seven years is still left unfulfilled. Daniel 9:26 predicts "a ruler will arise whose armies will destroy the city and the

Temple," referring to the Roman army of that day, which did come and destroy the city and the Temple in AD 70. But for the future ruler of the revived Roman Empire, his prophetic destiny during the last seven years awaits. The new leader of the revived Roman Empire will seize control of the nations led by an oligarchy of ten world leaders. With that power consolidated, he will then make his next decisive move. He will negotiate a peace covenant, guaranteeing Israel's security and bringing peace to the Middle East. According to Daniel, this important move will begin the last seven years of the predicted 490 years. It will be, in fact, the last seven years of world history before Armageddon and the second coming of Christ.

"He will confirm a covenant with many for one 'seven.' In the middle of the 'seven' he will put an end to sacrifice and offering. And on a wing of the temple he will set up an abomination that causes desolation, until the end that is decreed is poured out on him" (Daniel 9:27, NIV).

The world leader will move from a tactic of peace to a tactic of crushing power. As dictator of the revived Roman Empire, he will make peace with Israel, and he will keep his covenant during the first three and a half years of his rule. In the middle of the seven years, however, he will break his agreement. As noted in the previous chapter, this very possibly will coincide with Russia's attempt to invade Israel and Russia's mysterious annihilation. With the world balance of power dramatically in his favor and the world dazzled by the defeat of Russia and her Islamic allies, the Antichrist will show his true colors. He will declare himself world dictator and move to crush all opposition.

FORTY-TWO MONTHS OF HORROR

The prophets throughout the Bible have described the last years before the second coming of Christ as a time of great trouble. This is the time when the last world dictator will "devour the whole world, trampling and crushing everything in its path" (Daniel 7:23). Jesus described this time as one of "greater anguish than at any time since the world began.

And it will never be so great again. In fact, unless that time of calamity is shortened, not a single person will survive. But it will be shortened for the sake of God's chosen ones" (Matthew 24:21-22).

This is the same period and the same ruler described in Revelation 13. Revelation 13:5 tells us he will be given power and authority to reign for forty-two months. Revelation 13:7 reveals: "And the beast was allowed to wage war against God's holy people and to conquer them. And he was given authority to rule over every tribe and people and language and nation." Satan's man of destiny will have forty-two months of power as the world dictator. In the process of this rule, God will bring His terrible judgments on a wicked, Christ-rejecting world.

The prophetic calendar has been announced for centuries. The die is cast. The Middle East will return to the center of the international stage. The ten world leaders will emerge to consolidate the power lost by the fall of Rome. The future world dictator will await the right moment to upset three of these leaders and seize control of the Group of Ten, thereby controlling all the nations in the new European Union.

For three and a half years he will masquerade as a prince of peace, the savior of the world. For the next three and a half years he will use satanic wonders and power to declare himself god and ruthlessly crush all opposition.

Near the end of that period the nations of the world will field armies to challenge him. Gripped in a dramatic world war, the armies will converge to begin the suicidal Battle of Armageddon, as described in chapter 13.

TOOLS OF WORLD DOMINATION EXIST TODAY

It is most significant that in the twenty-first century not only does a need for a world government exist, but the tools for establishing such a government are now in our hands. Today the electronic media, especially use of television via satellite, is a tremendous tool that allows instant communication with the entire earth. CNN now reaches almost every corner of the world. Access to the Internet and satellite cell phones reach around the globe.

Missile warfare is also a tremendous tool to enforce world rule. Missiles can be fired and guided by GPS to almost any spot in the world in less than thirty minutes. A ruler with nuclear submarines and missiles at his disposal could threaten any portion of the world—blackmailing it into submission with the threat of extinction. No previous ruler in the history of the world has had such fearful weapons to enforce his rule.

In the field of economics, the Bible predicts that the world ruler will have absolute control of the economy, and no one will buy or sell without his permission (Revelation 13:17). Today, with the advent of electronic funds transfer, electronic banking, and widespread use of debit and credit cards, this is literally possible for the first time in world history. Large transfers of cash are already controlled by the government. Hundreds of millions of dollars move by wire every day in the international banking system. Credit and debit card transactions are verified in real time by phone, cell phone, and Internet access. At first the government control of the banking system might simply be a move to control the money used to finance terrorism or criminal activity. It is hard to imagine how international terrorism could be stopped without it.

Every person and business would have an account on the approved and government-controlled network. Everyone would be required to have a permanent identification number. Employers could only pay employees by electronic transfer of funds. All mortgages and utility bills—in fact, the sale or purchase of anything—would require such an account. When a person wanted to make a purchase, the store would simply check the person's account electronically and then subtract his or her purchases instantly by connecting to the system by phone or Internet.

In such a scenario currency and barter would be outlawed. The banks would recall all currency and simply issue credits to electronic accounts. If a world ruler chose to use such a system instead of money, no one could buy or sell unless the government provided an approved number, bar code, or mark. The government would have absolute economic control.

In our modern world all forms of representative and democratic governments will continue to be plagued by overwhelming problems. These will tend to undermine efforts at strong and resolute world leadership. As both domestic and international problems increase, the world will look for a new leader to act decisively to end the turmoil precipitated by events in the Middle East crisis and the threats to the world's oil supply. Both the need and the tools for the control of the world by one strong ruler exist today. The increasing availability of nuclear weapons, the propaganda power of the world media, and the blackmail power of international economic agreements and embargoes will make it possible for a world dictator to seize control of the world in a way that would have been impossible in any previous generation.

In an amazing way, the necessary ingredients for a world government are present for the first time in the history of civilization. The time may not be far away when such a government, foretold in Scripture, will have its accurate and complete fulfillment.

See how today's headlines relate to this chapter at *http://www.prophecyhotline.com.*

THE FINAL HOLOCAUST

EVENT #8: The world ruler breaks his peace with Israel, destroys the Temple in Jerusalem, and attempts to exterminate the Jewish people.

I am worried by the growing anti-Semitism and anti-Zionism in the world.

STEVEN SPIELBERG

BY ANY STANDARD THE JEWISH people have suffered more abuse and mistreatment than any group of people in human history. They have been the world's scapegoat. Stereotypes abound. And the virulent virus of anti-Semitism shows no signs of dying. In recent years it has simply mutated into a new strain. There's a powerful resurgence of anti-Semitism worldwide, especially in Europe, where it's being fueled by a growing population of Arab immigrants.

One outgrowth of anti-Semitism in recent years is a strange case of historical revisionism. As incredible as it may seem, some today are questioning if the Jewish Holocaust at the hands of the Nazis even occurred. Iranian president Mahmoud Ahmadinejad recently stated that the entire Jewish Holocaust is probably a myth, or if it did occur, it was greatly exaggerated.[1] Most of the world was appalled when he addressed a government-sponsored conference for Holocaust deniers and white supremacists that met in Tehran in December 2006. Afterward, he welcomed participants in his office, saying, "The Zionist regime will disappear soon." According to the *New York Times*, he "also suggested that the work of the government-sponsored conference—billed as a chance for 'both sides' on the Holocaust to be heard—should continue with the formation of a committee to determine whether the mass killings by Nazis of Jews and others really happened."[2]

THE NEW ANTI-SEMITISM

A new term has arisen in recent years to describe the modern rise in anti-Semitism. It's been termed "the new anti-Semitism." But what is the new anti-Semitism? How is it different from the old form?

The old anti-Semitism was hatred for the Jewish people and a desire to eradicate them. The new anti-Semitism is opposition to the very existence of a state for the Jewish people. It's a denial of Israel's right to exist and a desire to eradicate the Jewish state. Jews everywhere are now being held responsible for the military policies of the Israeli government. Jews and the existence of the state of Israel are being blamed for everything from terrorism to the threat of nuclear war in the Middle East.

The new anti-Semitism is interesting in light of Bible prophecy, which tells us that in the end times Israel will be hated by the nations of the earth. The Bible presents the coming tribulation period as a time of mounting opposition against Israel climaxing in an attack by all the nations of the earth.

Zechariah 12:2-3 says, "I will make Jerusalem like an intoxicating drink that makes the nearby nations stagger when they send their armies to besiege Jerusalem and Judah. On that day I will make Jerusalem an immovable rock. All the nations will gather against it to try to move it, but they will only hurt themselves."

In other words, while many nations will relish the idea of conquering Jerusalem, those who try to possess her will face disaster. Israel will be a heavy jagged stone that will cut to pieces those who try to remove her from her place. The frustration and hatred toward Israel in our world today are obvious. But what is behind all the animosity?

WHY THE WORLD HATES ISRAEL

Israel has been threatened repeatedly, particularly since the birth of the modern nation in 1948.[3] Scripture, particularly Revelation 12, reveals that the real source of opposition against Israel is Satan. As the enemy of the Jews and Jesus, their Messiah, he is the original source of anti-Semitism.

Satan has been on a mission to destroy the Jewish people and prevent the Messiah's coming ever since God promised Abraham that the Messiah would come through his line. Satan instigated several unsuccessful attempts to eradicate the Jewish people. First, Haman tried to wipe out the Jews in the days of Esther in about 480 BC. Next, the Syrian monarch Antiochus Epiphanes tried to destroy them in about 165 BC.

When those plans failed, Satan plotted to kill Christ. Satan tried to destroy Him right after His birth through the evil of King Herod (Matthew 2:16-18). When this failed, he inspired the Jewish and Roman leaders to kill the Son of God. However, he could not foresee the resurrection of Christ.

Now Satan is working on yet another plan. Once again, he is seeking ways to destroy the Jewish people over whom the Messiah is to rule. He made his greatest attempt to destroy the Jewish people under the Third Reich, when Adolph Hitler sent six million Jews to their death.

In the end times, the Antichrist will begin his career by acting like he is the great friend of Israel, but in the Great Tribulation he will slaughter the Jews mercilessly (Daniel 7:25; 8:24; 11:44). The Antichrist will be totally empowered, controlled, and motivated by Satan, so his persecution of Israel must be an expression of Satan's hatred for Israel (Revelation 13:4).

ISRAEL LETS DOWN HER GUARD

As a result of the coming peace treaty with the Antichrist, Israel will exhibit a new sense of security and lay down her weapons. For almost three and half years, peace for Israel will stand firm. But this era of peace and productivity will end when the coalition of nations described in Ezekiel 38 makes its final move into Israel. As we saw in chapter 7, this strike force will include Russia and her Islamic allies. In one of the great miracles of all history, God will supernaturally annihilate these invaders.

Apparently, the Antichrist will rise up during this time of mayhem and chaos to seize global control and position himself as the world's omnipotent ruler. His first order of business will be to secure Israel and the Middle East. In one of the great double-crosses of all time, the Antichrist will break his peace treaty with Israel at the midpoint of the seven-year agreement. The Antichrist will then attempt to finish what Hitler started. His goal will be nothing short of genocide, and he will almost succeed. Zechariah 13:8 says that two-thirds of the people of Israel will die and one-third will be left in the land.

THE COMING TIME OF TROUBLE FOR THE PEOPLE OF ISRAEL

Many end-time prophecies were given to Israel concerning a coming "time of trouble for my people Israel" or what's commonly called the "time of Jacob's trouble" (Jeremiah 30:7, KJV).

The first place this time of future tribulation is prophesied in the Bible is in Deuteronomy 4:30: "In the distant future, when you are suffering all these things, you will finally return to the LORD your God and listen to what he tells you." In Scripture this time of trouble is related to the end times when Israel will be regathered to her ancient land. The prophet Jeremiah records: "For the time is coming when I will restore the fortunes of my people of Israel and Judah. I will bring them home to this land that I gave to their ancestors, and they will possess it again. I, the LORD, have spoken!" (Jeremiah 30:3).

The Top 10 Prophecies of Israel's Future

1. Israel will be regathered and formed into a nation (Isaiah 43:5-6; Jeremiah 30:3; Ezekiel 34:11-13; 36:34; 37:1-14; Romans 11:25-27). Preparation for this began in May 1948 and continues to the present.

2. The Antichrist will make a seven-year treaty with Israel (Daniel 9:27).

3. The Jewish people will rebuild the Temple in Jerusalem (Matthew 24:15).

4. Russia and her Islamic allies will invade the nation of Israel when she is at peace (Ezekiel 38–39).

5. The Antichrist will invade Israel and desecrate the Temple (Matthew 24:15-20; 2 Thessalonians 2:4).

6. Many Jews will flee into the wilderness (Revelation 12:13-17).

7. During the Tribulation, two-thirds of the Jews will perish (Zechariah 13:8).

8. The armies of the world will gather in northern Israel at Megiddo (Revelation 16:12-16).

9. Jerusalem will be attacked and taken (Zechariah 12:1-9; 14:1-2).

10. Jesus Christ will return from heaven to defeat the armies of the world gathered in Israel, and many Jews will turn to Jesus as their Messiah (Zechariah 12:10; Revelation 19:19-21).

Immediately after this prediction of Israel's return is the description of her time of trouble. Israel is described as a woman experiencing the pains of childbirth. Her day of trouble is described in graphic terms in Jeremiah 30:7: "In all history there has never been such a time of terror. It will be a time of trouble for my people Israel. Yet in the end they will be saved!" On the basis of this promise, the progression or sequence of events as they relate to Israel in the end times will be her regathering, her time of trouble, and finally her time of deliverance when Christ returns.

We see the same basic order of events in Daniel's description of this future period. Key sections of Daniel's prophecy have already been

explained, and Daniel 11:40-45, which contains an important description of events at the end of the period, will be explained in chapter 13.
The prophet's concluding description of this period is given in Daniel
12:1: "At that time Michael, the archangel who stands guard over your
nation, will arise. Then there will be a time of anguish greater than any
since nations first came into existence. But at that time every one of
your people whose name is written in the book will be rescued." The
verses that immediately follow indicate that this will occur directly
before the second coming of Christ.

This great time of trouble for Israel will be the period just before
the second coming of Christ to the earth. In Daniel 7:25 and 12:7 it is
described as extending for "time, times, and half a time," or three and
a half years. This is in keeping with other prophecies of Daniel, such
as Daniel 9:27, where it is described as half of a seven-year period.
Revelation 12:6 speaks of the period as 1,260 days, or forty-two months
(Revelation 13:5). Brief though it may be, this three-and-a-half-year
period of great horror will include the most awful times of catastrophe and destruction that Israel and the entire world have ever known.
Many other passages in the Old Testament give additional descriptions,
such as Daniel 7:7-8 and the explanation of it in Daniel 7:19-27. The
Great Tribulation, according to Scripture, will be followed by a time
of glorious restoration for the Jewish people (see Joel 2:28-32; 3:17-
21; Zephaniah 3:14-18; Zechariah 13:8–14:21). The Old Testament
as a whole bears a clear witness to this climactic period of trouble that
is unprecedented in the entire history of the world but especially for
the Jewish people. The current problems facing Israel and the Jewish
people are only the beginning of this great time of trouble yet ahead.

GOD IS IN CONTROL

It's painful to discuss the second holocaust that the Jewish people will
endure in the final years of this age. However, the good news is that
God will use this terrible disaster to bring the Jewish people to faith in
Jesus as their Messiah. God will put them in the vice of judgment, and

as a result, many of the Jewish people will call out to Him for deliverance and salvation. Isaiah 64:1 records their future call to the Lord for rescue: "Oh, that you would burst from the heavens and come down! How the mountains would quake in your presence!" Even at His second coming, many of the Jewish people will look upon the pierced Messiah and receive Him as Savior (Zechariah 12:10).

Terrible times are ahead for Israel. But in the end God promises that millions of Jews will be saved. We can already see how the stage is being set for the fulfillment of these amazing prophecies.

 See how today's headlines relate to this chapter at
http://www.prophecyhotline.com.

CHAPTER 10

IRAQ: THE NEW BABYLON
ECONOMIC CENTER OF WORLD POWER

EVENT #9: The world ruler makes Iraq the new commercial and economic center of his world rule.

"The logistics alone are incredible, the cost, the . . . everything."
"What?"
"He wants to move the U.N."
"Move it?"
"Where?"
"It sounds stupid."
"Everything sounds stupid these days," Bailey said.
"He wants to move it to Babylon."
"You're not serious."
"He is."
"I hear they've been renovating that city for years. Millions of dollars invested in making it, what, New Babylon?"
"Billions. . . ."
"Within a year the United Nations headquarters will move to New Babylon."

TIM LAHAYE AND JERRY JENKINS,
LEFT BEHIND (A NOVEL)

WE ARE ALL PAINFULLY AWARE that Iraq has dominated U.S. foreign policy. The bloodshed and struggle over Iraq continues unabated.

It all started in 1990. Beginning in that year with the attack of Kuwait, Saddam Hussein became the world's public enemy number one. From that time until his capture, he did everything he could to harass and hinder Israel and the West, especially the United States.

The events during the first Gulf War in the early 1990s did not fulfill any specific biblical prophecies. But the subsequent invasion of Iraq and U.S. attempts to rebuild the city of Baghdad have created a scenario that requires reexamination of prophecy about the region. Does the rise of Iraq to world prominence have any significance for understanding end-time prophecy?[1]

BABYLON: CITY OF MAN

Jerusalem is the city that appears most often in the pages of the Bible. Jerusalem is mentioned just over 800 times. It is first named in Genesis 14 and last mentioned in Revelation 21. Jerusalem is consistently pictured in the Bible in a positive light. It is the city of God.

What many people may not realize is that the second most-mentioned city in the Bible is Babylon. The ancient city is located on the Euphrates River in modern Iraq near the Persian Gulf. Babylon is mentioned about 290 times in the Bible.

Babylon first appears in Genesis 10–11 and last appears in Revelation 17–18. Throughout the Bible, in contrast to Jerusalem, Babylon is pictured as man's city. It is consistently portrayed as a place of rebellion and pride. It was the first city built after the Flood. It was founded and ruled over by the world's first dictator, a man named Nimrod. It was the location of the famous Tower of Babel. From its inception Babylon was both a literal city and the false religious system that emanated from it. According to Revelation 17:5, "A mysterious name was written on her forehead: 'Babylon the Great, Mother of All Prostitutes and Obscenities in the World.'" Babylon, then, from its beginning is both a city and a system.

In Genesis 14, both Jerusalem (ancient Salem) and Babylon (ancient Shinar) are mentioned. They are total opposites. In this chapter, Babylon attacks Sodom and carries away its citizens, including Abraham's nephew Lot. When Abraham gets the news, he pursues Lot's captors and rescues his nephew. Melchizedek, the king of Salem, then comes out to bless Abraham.

From this point on in the Bible, we have what one might call "a tale of two cities." It's Jerusalem, God's city, versus Babylon, man's city. The story of these two cities takes us from the beginning to the end. It begins in Genesis and ends in Revelation.

In Revelation 17–18 Babylon is finally destroyed by God. In the final climax of world history, in Revelation 21, the New Jerusalem comes down out of heaven from God as the capital city of the new heaven and new earth and the eternal abode of God and His people.

That's a thumbnail sketch of the story of Babylon and Jerusalem from beginning to end. The basic lesson is simply this: Man's city falls, but God's city remains. Babylon is destroyed forever, but the heavenly city, the New Jerusalem, descends from heaven to endure forever.

With this basic blueprint in mind, let's take a closer look at a few of the details the Bible gives us about Babylon's history and destiny.

"FALLEN, FALLEN IS BABYLON THE GREAT!"

Most of the references in the Bible to Babylon concern the Babylonian empire that ruled the world of that day from 605–539 BC. King Nebuchadnezzar was the great leader of this empire. He invaded Judah three times. In the first invasion (605 BC), Daniel was taken captive. The second time the Babylonians came was in 597 when Ezekiel was carried away. Finally, in 586 Nebuchadnezzar's forces came and destroyed the great Temple of Solomon in Jerusalem.

Many of the prophets, including Isaiah, Jeremiah, Ezekiel, and Habakkuk, wrote about the Babylonians. This evil empire was the great menacing lion kingdom of sixth century BC (Jeremiah 4:7; Daniel 7:4).

The prophets warned Judah to repent or else God would send the Babylonians as an instrument of His discipline. However, once the Babylonians had come and destroyed the Temple, the message turned from one of judgment on Judah to hope for the future. Part of this message of comfort and hope was that God would repay Babylon for her sins. This message was intended to give God's people comfort, encouragement, and hope.

The Bible gives a detailed description of the destruction of Babylon in three key Old Testament passages: Isaiah 13; Isaiah 46–47; and Jeremiah 50–51.

Isaiah's Prophecy of Babylon's Final Destruction

Isaiah 13:4-5 says, "Hear the noise on the mountains! Listen, as the vast armies march! It is the noise and shouting of many nations. The LORD of Heaven's Armies has called this army together. They come from distant countries, from beyond the farthest horizons. They are the LORD's weapons to carry out his anger. With them he will destroy the whole land."

Isaiah continues in 13:10-13:

> *The heavens will be black above them;*
> *   the stars will give no light.*
> *The sun will be dark when it rises,*
> *   and the moon will provide no light.*
> *"I, the LORD, will punish the world for its evil*
> *   and the wicked for their sin.*
> *I will crush the arrogance of the proud*
> *   and humble the pride of the mighty.*
> *I will make people scarcer than gold—*
> *   more rare than the fine gold of Ophir.*
> *For I will shake the heavens.*
> *   The earth will move from its place*
> *when the LORD of Heaven's Armies displays his wrath*
> *   in the day of his fierce anger."*

In this chapter it appears that the prophet is looking down the corridors of time to the far destruction of Babylon in the end times since nothing like this happened to Babylon in the past. Jesus even referred to Isaiah 13:10 in Matthew 24:29 when He described the stellar signs that will accompany His second coming to earth.

The prophet also seems to refer to the far view, that is, the destruction of Babylon in relation to the second coming of Christ, in Isaiah 13:20-22, which says,

> *Babylon will never be inhabited again.*
> *It will remain empty for generation after generation.*
> *Nomads will refuse to camp there,*
> *and shepherds will not bed down their sheep.*
> *Desert animals will move into the ruined city,*
> *and the houses will be haunted by howling creatures.*
> *Owls will live among the ruins,*
> *and wild goats will go there to dance.*
> *Hyenas will howl in its fortresses,*
> *and jackals will make dens in its luxurious palaces.*
> *Babylon's days are numbered;*
> *its time of destruction will soon arrive.*

Isaiah 13:19 even says that when Babylon is finally destroyed it will be like Sodom and Gomorrah. "Babylon, the most glorious of kingdoms, the flower of Chaldean pride, will be devastated like Sodom and Gomorrah when God destroyed them."

As far as the historic fulfillment of these verses is concerned, it is obvious from both Scripture and history that these verses have not been literally fulfilled. The city of Babylon has never been destroyed suddenly and cataclysmically like Isaiah 13 describes. Babylon continued to flourish after the Medes conquered it under the leadership of Cyrus. When the Persians under King Cyrus conquered Babylon in 539 BC the city wasn't even destroyed. Though its glory dwindled, especially after the control of the Medes and Persians ended in 323 BC, the city continued in some form or substance until AD 1000 and did not experience a sudden, cataclysmic termination such as is anticipated in this prophecy.

Since nothing like this ever happened to the city of Babylon in its long and storied history, and since the Bible is God's Word and must be literally fulfilled, then we must conclude that it's a future event. And there's only one time in man's history when all this will occur: at the end of the future tribulation period in conjunction with the second coming of Jesus Christ.

Armageddon Brings Babylon's Destruction

Isaiah 14 seems to further confirm that the city's ultimate destruction is related to the second advent of Christ and the Day of the Lord. The satanic power behind Babylon, addressed as "Lucifer, son of the morning" (Isaiah 14:12, NKJV), is portrayed both in his original rebellion against God and in his ultimate judgment. The destruction of Babylon is related to the time of final restoration for the Jewish people (Isaiah 14:1-3) and the judgment upon the rulers of the nations (Isaiah 14:4-7).

The final Old Testament prophecy about Babylon is found in Zechariah 5:5-11. This prophecy also indicates that Babylon will be rebuilt in the end times.

In Zechariah 5, the prophet Zechariah sees a vision of a basket that is full of wickedness, personified as a woman. A heavy lid is put on the basket to keep the evil in check. God doesn't want the wickedness to get out. As Zechariah sees the basket being carried away, he asks where the basket is being taken. The angel replies, "To the land of Babylonia, where they will build a temple for the basket. And when the temple is ready, they will set the basket there on its pedestal" (5:11).

When Zechariah wrote these words, the Babylonian empire had already been conquered by the Medo-Persians about twenty-five years earlier. And there is no event after Zechariah's prophecy that could be legitimately seen as the fulfillment of this prophecy. So what does this mean? It means that Zechariah's prophecy is still in the future. It means that someday, when the necessary preparations have been made, wickedness again will be focused in the land of Babylon. Wickedness will rear its ugly head in the place of its origin—Babylon.

The Bible indicates that history will come full circle in the end times and that Babylon will be the headquarters for the final world ruler, the Antichrist (Revelation 17–18). The city of Babylon has never been completely destroyed as the Bible predicts in such passages as Isaiah 13 and Jeremiah 50–51. These texts indicate that Babylon will be wiped out like Sodom and Gomorrah, that no brick from the city will ever be used again, that no one will ever live there, and that the city will never be rebuilt. For these passages to be literally fulfilled, Babylon must be rebuilt to all its former glory and destroyed once and for all at the end of the time of great horror.

BABYLON IN THE END TIMES

In the final mention of Babylon in Revelation 17–18, the city of man is symbolized by a seductive harlot riding on the back of the Antichrist, who is symbolized by a wild beast. This connection between Babylon and the Beast, or the Antichrist, indicates that the two will be closely allied. Babylon in the end times, like Babylon in the beginning, will be both a false religious system and a literal city on the Euphrates River that will serve as an economic and commercial capital for the Antichrist.

Revelation 17 seems to focus on the religious aspect of Babylon, while Revelation 18 focuses on the city's political and economic characteristics. Revelation 17 depicts the destruction of the Babylonian false religious system by the Antichrist and his henchmen at the midpoint of the seven-year Tribulation.

The New Superchurch

This false religious system is probably a kind of "superchurch" or world church that will pull together people of various religious backgrounds into one great ecclesiastical alliance. It will probably be centered in the restored, rebuilt city of Babylon.

Even now, we see hints of what this may be like, as a number of people in the church deny some of the central tenets of the faith. This is not surprising, given the movement toward a world church within Protestant Christianity during the last century. When the World Council of Churches was organized in Amsterdam in 1948, one of its aims was to bring all branches of Christianity, including Protestant, Roman Catholic, and Eastern Orthodox churches, under one organization. In the process, strict adherence to biblical doctrine and orthodox theology was sacrificed for organizational unity. Church leaders weren't engaged in minor disputes over some fine point of theology but over the central doctrine of Jesus Christ—who He was and what He did when He died upon the cross.

Disputes in theology are not new, and departures from strict adherence to biblical truth have occurred throughout the centuries, beginning in the days of the apostles (see 2 Peter 2:1-2; 2 Peter 3:3-4; 2 Timothy 4:2-4). In the past century, however, changes in theology have been more rapid and more devastating to biblical faith than ever before. The belief that the Bible is the Word of God has been abandoned by many within the church.

The Disappearance of True Believers

Yet the Bible makes clear that the situation will be far worse in the end times. The Holy Spirit, who now restrains evil in the world and who indwells the church, will be taken away at the time of the Rapture. In other words, the Spirit's restraining influence through the Church will be removed (2 Thessalonians 2:6-7). Obviously the removal of every Christian in the world who is indwelt by the Spirit will release a flood tide of evil such as the world has never seen. It will allow the immediate takeover of the world church by those completely devoid of Christian faith and will allow other forces of evil a free hand in human history.

Fear and panic will accompany the disappearance of true believers from the earth at the time of the Rapture (1 Thessalonians 4:13-18). This will amplify the world's desire for a strong religious organization to bring order from that religious chaos. With millions of people disappearing, natural disasters, a rapid rise in demonic power, and false prophets performing signs and wonders, the world will be grasping for something that is secure. In desperation the masses will turn to the world church for help.

Without the redeeming presence of true believers, people from all kinds of religious background or no religious background will combine into a powerful religious and political institution. This superchurch will have power to put to death those who resist its demands for adherence (Revelation 17:6). The new world church will be in alliance with the political powers of the reunited Roman Empire. This combined effort will prepare the way for a new government with absolute power over the entire world. This unholy alliance is portrayed symbolically in Revelation 17, which describes a wicked harlot riding a scarlet-colored beast.

False Religion and False Peace

For centuries expositors have recognized the harlot as the symbol of false religion and the scarlet beast as representing the political power of the revived Roman Empire in the end times. While their alliance will bring a temporary stability to the world, it will also create a blasphemous religious system that will lead the world to new depths of immorality and departure from true faith in God.

One of the fruits of their combined power will be the forced peace with Israel. While there will be some show of religious tolerance in permitting the revival of Judaism, it will be short-lived and will continue only as long as the peace treaty is observed. In other parts of the world, persecution and martyrdom will follow the extending power of the combined political and ecclesiastical alliance. But the final form of world religion will emerge later.

The Group of Ten and the Antichrist will use this false religious system as long as it serves their interests. However, at the midpoint of the Tribulation, the Antichrist and the Group of Ten will no longer need the power and help of the superchurch. The Antichrist will destroy this false religious system and replace it with his own ecclesiastical apostasy, the final form of religious wickedness, the worship of himself (Revelation 17:16-17).

"After All This"

Revelation 18 begins with the words "After all this" ("And after these things" in the King James Version). This indicates that Revelation 18 records events that will follow the fall of the religious harlot or super-church during the middle of the Tribulation. Revelation 18 focuses on the political and economic system centered in Babylon that will reach its zenith under the rule of the Antichrist.

The description of the sins of Babylon as "piled as high as heaven" (Revelation 18:5) is an unmistakable allusion back to the Tower of Babel, whose bricks were piled up toward heaven (Genesis 11:5-9). This marked the beginning of the pride, selfishness, and greed associated with the ancient political and economic world capital in Babylon. When the Antichrist makes Babylon his capital, the city will seem invincible. But the sin of this city will be piled up, and God will bring the Antichrist's enemies against the city to burn her with fire.

Revelation 18 prophesies the final destruction of the city of Babylon just before the second coming of Jesus Christ in Revelation 19:11-21. When Babylon falls suddenly and unexpectedly, the leaders and merchants of the world will marvel and be terrified at the destruction of the great city (Revelation 18:9-19). Babylon's fall will be a dreaded omen of the total unraveling of the Antichrist's world empire. It is significant that the final destruction on earth before Jesus returns will be the razing of Babylon, man's city.

BABYLON BACK IN THE NEWS

Four key factors indicate that Babylon could quickly become the city described in end-time prophecy:

First, Saddam Hussein began renovating the ancient city while in power. While the rebuilding is far from complete, the fact that it even began is intriguing. During Operation Iraqi Freedom and for several years after, American troops were stationed in the city of Babylon in a place appropriately named "Camp Babylon." Many military ceremonies were held there.

Fifty miles to the north, the United States has begun a massive project to build and staff a fortress-like embassy complex beside the Tigris River in Baghdad. The embassy, known as "Embassy Baghdad," is the largest of its kind in the world—the size of Vatican City, with a population of 5,500. The embassy complex covers 104 acres and includes 21 buildings. It dwarfs U.S. embassies elsewhere that typically cover about 10 acres. The Baghdad embassy has its own defense force and self-contained power and water.

USA Today provided this description of "Embassy Baghdad":

> The massive new embassy, being built on the banks of the Tigris River, is designed to be entirely self-sufficient and won't be dependent on Iraq's unreliable public utilities.
>
> The 104-acre complex—the size of about 80 football fields—will include two office buildings, one of them designed for future use as a school, six apartment buildings, a gym, a pool, a food court, and its own power generation and water-treatment plants. The average Baghdad home has electricity only four hours a day, according to Bowen's office. The current U.S. Embassy in Iraq has nearly 1,000 Americans working there, more than at any other U.S. embassy.[2]

Some worry that this massive symbol of U.S. presence in Iraq sends the wrong signal to the Iraqi people. But could it be that Embassy Baghdad is another key step toward the rise of Babylon?

Saddam Hussein compared himself to Nebuchadnezzar and began rebuilding Babylon. The United States has focused the resources of the wealthiest and most powerful country in the world on the task. The construction of this massive embassy in Baghdad could signal the beginning of a long-term Western presence in Iraq. Embassy Baghdad could easily be a first step for other Western powers to join in to rebuild a "New Babylon," preparing the city for its role in end-time events.

Second, Iraq sits on the fourth largest known crude oil reserves in the world (estimated at 115 billion barrels, compared to Saudi Arabia with about 266 billion barrels). However, some believe that Iraq may have as much as 300 billion barrels or 30 percent of the known reserves in the world. Iraq's actual oil reserves are still unknown since, according to the U.S. Energy Information Administration, 90 percent of Iraq's regions are unexplored. No one really knows how much oil Iraq has. Consider this. There are only 2,000 wells in all of Iraq compared with one million in Texas alone.[3] Just next door to Iraq, tiny Kuwait has 10 percent of the proven oil reserves.

The ousting of Saddam from power has resulted in a lifting of the sanctions and limitations on Iraqi oil sales. In the years ahead, one could expect that billions of dollars, euros, and yen will flood into Iraq. Western companies are salivating over Iraq's petroleum potential. Oil experts believe that with improved, modernized infrastructure, Iraq could easily pump out four million barrels a day. And this number could skyrocket if more reserves are discovered.[4] Future oil revenues and attempts to rebuild and stabilize Iraq by the United States and the West point to the rebuilding of Babylon as a major economic center for the Middle East.

Third, due to the war there, Iraq has become and continues to be a major focal point in the Middle East and Persian Gulf. With mounting casualties and the growing sense that the United States and its allies are stuck in a quagmire, many are now wondering if the war there will ever end. The answer is yes, at some time, because the Bible predicts that Babylon will become a world headquarters for the Antichrist. We don't know when or how it will finally grind to a halt, but as the war there continues to drag on, the United States will be forced to step up pressure on the Iraqis to get their government on track. If some degree of stability and security can be achieved, other nations will move quickly to Iraq to get a piece of this developing, oil-rich nation.

Fourth, the symbolic and strategic reasons for the Antichrist locating a capital city in Babylon would be powerful. What better place for the Antichrist to locate a major economic center than Babylon? It's in the geographical center of the Persian Gulf area surrounded by rich oil reserves. It's not far from Iraq's borders with Iran, Kuwait, and Saudi Arabia, affording a strategic location between these four oil-rich nations. Also, as the oil reserves of other Middle Eastern nations are being drained by millions of barrels a day, Iraq's vast reserves are hardly being touched. Iraq's huge oil reserves are sitting on the sidelines in the world's scramble for energy. In the next decade, as Iraq's oil potential is explored and ready to come online, Iraq could be poised to emerge as *the* oil giant. It could also be this buried treasure that leads the Antichrist to put his headquarters in Babylon so he can control the vast oil reserves of the world.[5]

Babylon also has symbolic significance. It was the ancient capital of King Nebuchadnezzar. It is the place where Alexander the Great died in 323 BC, and he had intended to make it his eastern capital.

The symbolism of such a move would be significant. The Antichrist will put his eastern capital in Babylon and control the main oil fields of the world. Just like Alexander the Great, the Antichrist will attempt to show his power over the world economy by making Babylon the center of his world rule.

While we don't know exactly how Babylon will be rebuilt or what will motivate men to carry out this task, the Bible says it will occur. And current events seem to indicate that it could be soon.

ANOTHER PIECE OF THE PUZZLE

Knowing what the Bible says about Babylon in the end times, we shouldn't be surprised by the rise of Iraq. This rise could serve as a perfect prelude for the building of Babylon in the near future. It's interesting that Iraq has come out of relative obscurity in the past twenty years to play a significant role in the world. The rise of Iraq to world prominence and the ongoing conflict are not accidents. The staggering oil wealth of Iraq is not just a stroke of good fortune. The resurgence of Iraq, the efforts that have already been made to restore and rebuild Babylon, and the rich oil reserves available to finance the rebuilding of the city all make the picture the Bible paints for Babylon in the end times very realistic.

Iraq occupies a pivotal role in the world today and in God's prophetic program. The headlines about Iraq are another part of the rapidly developing matrix of events in the Middle East that are setting the stage for the final end-time events predicted in God's Word.

See how today's headlines relate to this chapter at
http://www.prophecyhotline.com.

CHINA FLEXES ITS AWESOME POWER

EVENT #10: The dragon of Asia, starved for oil and economic growth, challenges the world ruler's control of the Middle East.

China's explosive growth could be the dominant event of this century. Never before has a country risen as fast as China is doing.

STAPLETON ROY, FORMER U.S. AMBASSADOR TO CHINA

ONE OF THE COLOSSAL DEVELOPMENTS of the twenty-first century is the political and military awakening of Asia—especially China. The great nations of Asia east of the Euphrates River, slumbering for centuries, are now beginning to stir and become a major factor in the international, socioeconomic, and political dynamics. The immensity of their geography and population make their development especially significant.

The People's Republic of China, with a population of 1.3 billion, is flexing its muscles around the globe. And most of this has taken place in the last twenty-five years. China's economic growth and power are rapidly accelerating. Even if there were no Scripture hinting at the place of China in end-time events, it would only be natural to expect them to be part of the worldwide scene in the end times.

149

THE CHINESE CENTURY

The June 20, 2005, cover story in *U.S. News & World Report* is titled: "The China Challenge." The article notes that China's economy is growing faster than that of any other nation in modern history. Soon it will become the world's second-largest purchaser of oil and leading buyer of cars, computers, and appliances. "Perhaps more important," the article continues, "China today is infused with a profound sense of destiny, a steely determination to regain primacy in world affairs. The rest of the world is just beginning to digest what that might mean."[1] *Time* also ran a cover story on this nation, called "China: Dawn of a New Dynasty," in January 2007. Reporter Michael Elliott writes: "China is aiming to become the world's greatest power."[2]

Consider these statistics on China's phenomenal rate of growth drawn from the two articles:

- China's economy is growing at a staggering 10 percent per year.
- China's economy will become the second largest in the world by 2020 (surpassing Japan and behind only the United States).
- China has sixteen of the world's most polluted cities.
- An estimated two million people in China have a net worth of at least forty million dollars.
- In 2003 China had 269 million cell phone users; there will be 500 million in 2008.
- China's military budget is the third largest in the world. China has cash for missiles, satellites, and other advanced weapons.
- Military spending has increased 300 percent in the last decade.
- China still regards Taiwan as a renegade province.
- Chinese nationalism is on the rise. The Chinese want to reclaim the grandeur of their past.
- The trade gap between China and the United States is growing by 25 percent per year. Last year Americans spent $162 billion more on Chinese products than the Chinese spent on U.S. products.

The 2006 *Quadrennial Defense Review* released by the Pentagon described China as possessing "the greatest potential to compete militarily with the United States and field disruptive military technologies that over time offset traditional U.S. military advantages."[3] In fact, the anticipated growth of China's influence has already led many to dub this "the Chinese century." Undoubtedly, China will be a key international player to reckon with in the years ahead.

"CHINDIA"

Another country experiencing exponential growth is India. Some experts have coined a new term to denote this new combined world power—*Chindia*. Together, China and India have a combined population of 2.3 billion! Experts predict a mega boom there that will dwarf anything one can imagine. According to an article posted at Bloomberg.com, "The combined gross domestic production of China and India may be $16 trillion a year by 2020. . . . The two nations may account for 17 percent of world GDP by then, up from 7 percent now."[4] A 5 percent increase in anything there, such as cars or cell phones, is the equivalent of a 40 percent increase in the United States simply because they have eight times as many people.[5]

One expert says that, "Chindia will be the main event—almost the only show on the planet—for perhaps the rest of your life."[6]

The combined Chinese and Indian economies will have staggering global effects.

FUELING THE DRAGON

One of the most dramatic results of the rise of China is its influence on world oil markets. China is already the world's second largest consumer of oil, and its consumption increases by 7.5 percent a year, seven times faster than the United States. By 2010 China will have ninety times more cars than it had in 1990. At the current rate of growth, China's thirst for oil will increase by 150 percent by 2020. China's oil imports doubled from 2000 to 2005. If China's oil imports keep rising at the current rate, its oil demand by 2025 would be 21 million barrels a day, matching current U.S. consumption.[7] By 2030, it's projected that the number of cars in China will surpass that in the United States. What does this mean?

China has no long-standing strategic interests in the Middle East, but China is quickly cultivating ties with Saudi Arabia. In light of its exploding economy and need for oil, the Chinese are now scouring the earth for black gold.

China has entered into a series of agreements with Venezuela, which is America's fourth largest oil supplier, to give China a greater share of Venezuelan oil. Chinese state-owned companies are also seeking ambitious deals in Canada, which is another key U.S. supplier. China's third largest oil producer even made an ill-fated, hostile bid for the American oil company Unocal in 2005. The China Petrochemical Corporation has made a deal with Iran worth $100 billion to develop Iran's Yadavaran oil fields.

China is doing all it can to curry favor with Iran and keep the oil flowing. China holds one of the five permanent seats on the United Nations Security Council, and the Chinese have consistently obstructed any meaningful sanctions against Iran for its nuclear ambitions. Also, in the 1990s, China began selling sophisticated missiles to Iran, and Iran has passed these missiles on to Hezbollah. During Israel's war with Hezbollah in the summer of 2006, the Israeli warship *Hanit* was hit by an Iranian-made variant of a Chinese antiship missile.

Clearly, China is actively pursuing every opportunity to secure her energy resources for the future. Chinese officials already know what's finally beginning to dawn on everyone else—China's growing appetite for oil will be insatiable as her economy explodes. Here's one more fact about China's impact on the world oil market. At present about 58 percent of China's oil imports come from the Middle East, but by 2015 about 70 percent of her oil must come from that region.

All this will have a dramatic impact in at least three ways. First, China will continue to expand and siphon off more and more of the available crude from Iran, Russia, and the world market. Second, it will further concentrate the United States' and Europe's attention on the Middle East, as they will become more dependent than ever on oil from key allies in the Middle East. And third, because of its rapid growth, China will inevitably be forced to compete directly with the West for the oil in the Middle East.

DANIEL'S PROPHECY OF AN INVASION FROM THE EAST

The meteoric rise of China from a backward communist nation to an economic and military juggernaut appears to fit in with the biblical alignment of nations in the end times. The Bible predicts that world power will be divided into four main geographical regions. This alignment of nations is described by the directions on the compass in relation to the nation of Israel. To the north is Russia, along with Turkey and Iran. The southern region includes the modern Islamic nations of Egypt, Libya, and Sudan. The western region contains the kingdom of the Antichrist—centered in the reunited Roman Empire. The nations east of the Euphrates River invade the Middle East in the end times (Revelation 16:12-14).

Students of Bible prophecy have long believed that China would be the leader of this great eastern power. What we see happening there today is staggering. The transformation is radical and accelerating. One could easily see how this great rising power will be the final great kingdom standing to challenge the power of the Antichrist. Prophecies in Daniel 11, along with Revelation 9 and 16, paint a vivid picture of what is expected to happen right before the Battle of Armageddon.

In Daniel's prophecy of "the time of the end" beginning in Daniel 11:35, a king is pictured in the Mediterranean who engages in a military conflict with the king of the south, the king of the north, and a military force from the east. This king, who by this point will have assumed the role of a world dictator, is the head of the revived Roman Empire. In the latter part of the Great Tribulation, just prior to the second coming of Christ, major portions of the world will rebel against him. This explains the military conflict with armies pushing against him from the south, the north, and the east.

The prophecy in Daniel 11:44 says, "But then news from the east and the north will alarm him, and he will set out in great anger to destroy and obliterate many." Although we aren't given every detail, it appears that this news concerns a military invasion from the Far East. This is probably the first word of trouble in the Far East related to the Antichrist's worldwide empire and comes as an added blow to the insurrection in the north and the south.

But the conflict with the armies of the north and south is not completely resolved as the armies from the east join the melee. At the time of the second coming of Christ a great war is underway in which the armies are deployed over much of the Holy Land with the valley of Armageddon as its focal point.

This passage in Daniel, however, explains that nations from the east will have a place in the great world conflict of the end times.

The 200 Million Man March

Two important passages in Revelation, namely 9:13-21 and 16:12-16, also suggest that one of the large armies employed in the final world conflict will be a military force of great power from China. The first hint of this is found in Revelation 9, where the apostle John says:

> Then the sixth angel blew his trumpet, and I heard a voice speaking from the four horns of the gold altar that stands in the presence of God. And the voice said to the sixth angel who held the trumpet, "Release the four angels who are bound at the great Euphrates River." Then the four angels who had been prepared for this hour and day and month and year were turned loose to kill one-third of all the people on earth. I heard the size of their army, which was 200 million mounted troops. (Revelation 9:13-16)

The passage goes on to describe the character of this army and the fact that one-third of the world's population was killed in the resulting military struggle.

Although all of the details are not entirely clear, the most reasonable explanation of this prophecy, related as it is to the great Euphrates River that forms the eastern boundary of the ancient Roman Empire, is that the army comes from the Far East and crosses the Euphrates River in order to participate in the struggle that is going on in the land of Israel. The statement that it is "prepared for this hour and day and month and year were turned loose to kill one-third of all the people on earth" means simply that special angels had been prepared to unleash an army for the day of battle that follows.

The most staggering statistic is the fact that the number of the army is declared to be two hundred million. Never in the history of the human race until now has there been an army of this size. The total number of men under arms in World War II on both sides of the conflict combined was never more than fifty million. Therefore, many have been tempted to spiritualize the number or to regard the army as demonic rather than human. The statistics of two hundred million horsemen must have been especially astounding to the apostle John, for at that time the total world population did not exceed this number.

With the advent of the twenty-first century, an army of two hundred million men from the east becomes increasingly possible. For the first time in history such an army is plausible. If such an army is to be raised up, it would be natural to conclude that it would come from China and possibly India, the great population centers of the world. It's fascinating that China alone claims to have more than two hundred million men and women fit for military service, the figure mentioned in Revelation 9:16.[8]

Although their militia includes the home guard, which under present circumstances would not be thrown into a battle such as the one in Revelation, it at least introduces the possibility that the number should be taken literally. If so, this is an imposing statistic of the power and influence of China in the final world war. The deadly character of the army is revealed in their slaughter of one-third of the world's population, a figure mentioned in Revelation 9:15 and again in Revelation 9:18.

A third biblical reference related to China in the end times is found in the sixth bowl judgment described in Revelation 16:12, which says, "Then the sixth angel poured out his bowl on the great Euphrates River, and it dried up so that the kings from the east could march their armies toward the west without hindrance." Revelation 16:14 (NIV) reveals that this movement is part of a worldwide gathering of "the kings of the whole world" in order that they might participate in "the battle on the great day of God Almighty." According to Revelation 16:16, the geographical focal point of the gathering is Armageddon (Mount Megiddo in northern Israel).

The most simple and suitable explanation for understanding "the kings from the east" (Revelation 16:12) is to take the passage literally. The Euphrates River then becomes the geographic boundary of the ancient Roman Empire. The kings of the east are kings from the east or "of the sun rising"; that is, monarchs who originate in the Far East. The battle that ensues is therefore a genuine military conflict.

The interpretation of Revelation 16:12, if taken literally, provides an important piece of information concerning the final world conflict. According to this verse, the invasion from the east starts by an act of God in drying up the Euphrates River. This miraculous drying up of the Euphrates River permits easy access for the descent of the tremendous army of two hundred million men from China upon the land of Israel. This act of God will allow the army to cross the dry riverbed just as the children of Israel were able to walk on dry land when they reached the Red Sea and the Jordan River.

From the standpoint of Scripture, the Euphrates is one of the important rivers of the world. The first reference is found in Genesis 2:10-14, where it is mentioned as one of the four rivers having its source in the Garden of Eden. The Euphrates River is mentioned a total of nineteen times in the Old Testament and twice in the New Testament. In Genesis 15:18 it is described as the eastern boundary of the land promised to Israel. An army, therefore, that crosses the Euphrates River from the east to the west invades the Promised Land.

The Euphrates River has long been an important geographic barrier, and in the ancient world it was second to none in importance. Its total length is some seventeen hundred miles, and it is the main river of southwestern Asia, dividing the land geographically much as the Mississippi River divides North America. Not only from the standpoint of prophecy, but historically, geographically, and biblically the Euphrates River is the most important in the ancient world. To take the Revelation 16 passage literally makes perfect sense.

It makes sense to interpret the phrase "the kings of the east" literally as well. After all, one could reasonably expect that nations from the Far East would be involved in a world war culminating in the oil-rich Middle East. Thus, identifying the kings of the east with China, and possibly other nations such as India, fits the biblical evidence.

China's Middle East Move

One final question concerning China: Why would China, and possibly other nations such as India, move into Israel in the end times? The Bible never says specifically why the kings of the east make their move, but it appears that China's final great invasion is against the Roman ruler or the Antichrist. As we have already seen, in the end times the Antichrist will establish his headquarters in Babylon right in the middle of the world's great oil producers (Saudi Arabia, Iraq, Iran, and Kuwait).

By strategically positioning himself in this location, the Antichrist will exercise domination over the Middle East and its oil reserves. By controlling this part of the world, he could easily strangle other nations into submission by means of oil blackmail.

With this picture in mind, one can easily imagine what will happen. As the Great Tribulation lurches to its climax, China and other nations east of the Euphrates will tire of the Antichrist's control of the world's oil supply and will decide to make their final move for survival. They will have no other choice. Oil will be the lifeblood of their civilization.

As this advancing horde drives westward, they will capture and destroy Babylon as recorded in Revelation 18. By this act, they will destroy the Antichrist's great city and secure control over the oil supply they desperately covet. By this time the Antichrist will have retreated to Israel, so the great eastern army will advance to Israel for the final showdown of east versus west. The horrific clash of armies comes at Armageddon in northern Israel. During the final act of this drama Christ will interrupt this conflict with His second coming to earth. He will destroy the Antichrist and all the armies gathered at Armageddon (Revelation 19:11-21).

China intends to dominate the world in the twenty-first century. Its rapid economic growth requires more and more oil and inevitably puts it in competition with the West. It is not surprising that the Antichrist's bid to dominate the world from Babylon will inevitably be challenged by the nations east of the Euphrates River. In China, as in other parts of the world, the stage is being set for the final drama in which the kings of the east will fulfill their important role in end-time events.

See how today's headlines relate to this chapter at
http://www.prophecyhotline.com.

CHAPTER 12

NATURAL DISASTERS, DISEASE, AND FAMINE REACH EVERYONE

EVENT #11: Billions die in the worst series of disasters in the history of the world.

If you look over behind me, that's a tornado. Yes! A twister in Los Angeles. It's one of many tornadoes that are destroying our city. There's another one! That's the Los Angeles skyline! It's unbelievable! It's huge! I've never seen anything like that.

The Day After Tomorrow (2004)

MANY SIGNS TODAY POINT TO imminent, worldwide catastrophe. Even the most casual observers seem to be taking note of the actual and potential disasters the world faces. In one generation mankind has moved from apparent self-sufficiency to a feeling of impotence in the face of mounting world problems. In addition to fears about nuclear arsenals, dirty bombs, terrorists, and increasing pollution, in the twenty-first century natural disasters such as tsunamis, earthquakes, and hurricanes of unparalleled magnitude are occurring with frightening regularity. Add to this the real threat of an imminent, worldwide plague that could wipe out millions. It is easy to imagine how terrible disasters could accelerate in frequency and converge on the globe at the same time. People everywhere are wondering if these events could be signs of the times. Does the Bible have anything to say about natural disasters and deadly plagues in the end times?

HURRICANES, TSUNAMIS, AND EARTHQUAKES

Even people with little or no interest in Bible prophecy are suddenly wondering if all the natural disasters in the world signal that we are getting near "closing time." On December 26, 2004, Asia experienced an unparalleled tsunami, the worst natural disaster in recorded human history. The catastrophe left at least 200,000 dead and millions homeless. Then only a few months later in August 2005, the U.S. Gulf Coast was ravaged by Hurricane Katrina, the worst natural disaster in U.S. history, which wiped out a major American city. Katrina was followed quickly by Hurricane Rita, which also wreaked havoc along the Gulf Coast.

On October 8, 2005, a 7.6 magnitude earthquake—the same intensity as the 1906 San Francisco earthquake—rattled Pakistan, killing about 75,000 and injuring over 100,000. The tremor left 3.3 million people homeless and directly affected the lives of four million people.

Jesus Himself predicted that this present age would be marked by upheavals in nature and terrible plagues (Matthew 24:7; Luke 21:11). These are general signs, which mark the entire course of the present age between the two comings of Christ. However, like birth pangs, they will relentlessly grow in intensity and frequency in wave after wave of crippling contractions, indicating that the end of the age is approaching (Matthew 24:8; 1 Thessalonians 5:3).

What we are witnessing today gives a frightening preview of what's coming during the end times when these disasters intensify and go global.

PANDEMIC SUPERFLU

The recent spate of new diseases is nothing short of alarming. There have been so many new diseases emerging, it's difficult to keep up with them all. There's Ebola, West Nile virus, Lyme disease, mad cow disease, SARS, and Asia's newest threat—bird flu. The human death toll from the Asia bird flu is still not significant, but U.N. officials warn that the outbreak is far from over. The disease has killed people in nine countries, including Azerbaijan, Cambodia, Indonesia, China, Vietnam, and Thailand. But it is being battled in Japan, Laos, Pakistan, South Korea, Malaysia, and Russia. The specific strain of bird flu in Taiwan and Pakistan is different from the one in the other countries.

All of these new diseases come on the heels of the AIDS virus, one of the most destructive plagues the world has ever seen. Over 25 million people have died of AIDS since 1981, and 3.1 million died in 2005 alone. And just think, in the 1970s scientists believed they had basically conquered these kinds of diseases. The sudden and continuing outbreak of new diseases is astounding.

Jesus warned that worldwide plagues would portend His return to planet earth. In Luke 21:11 Jesus said, "There will be great earthquakes, and there will be famines and plagues in many lands, and there will be terrifying things and great miraculous signs from heaven."

There are growing concerns that a flu virus similar to the 1918 virus will move from birds to the human population and cause cataclysmic destruction. In the article "Flu Hope, or Horror?" editorialist Charles Krauthammer reports that the 1918 Spanish flu virus that caused a horrible pandemic was recreated by scientists recently. This virus was a bird flu. Krauthammer notes that "when the re-created virus was given to mice in heavily quarantined laboratories in Atlanta it killed the mice more quickly than any other flu virus ever tested."[1]

National Geographic's October 2005 cover article was titled "The Next Killer Flu: Can We Stop It?" It predicts, "Sooner or later a deadly virus that can jump from birds to people will sweep the globe." The article adds that the world is overdue for a flu pandemic. A new flu virus spread throughout the world's population three times in the twentieth century.

In 1918–1919 the "Spanish" flu killed an estimated 50 to 100 million people. *National Geographic* says that the virus "swept the globe in 1918 and early 1919. Except for a few Pacific Islanders, everyone on Earth was exposed to the disease, and half got sick."[2] Just think about that. Everyone on the earth was exposed to the disease. And that was long before jet air travel and the age of globalism. Second, the Asian flu, a mixture of bird and human viruses originating in southern China, killed one million people in 1957. Finally, the Hong Kong flu (also a mixture of bird and human viruses that killed about 750,000 people) struck in 1968.

What will happen in the twenty-first century? The article says that the H5N1 virus that is killing poultry and a few people in Asia could be the next global pandemic if it gains the ability to quickly spread from person to person. Incredibly, it is estimated that deaths from such a widespread pandemic could range from a conservative "7.4 million to an apocalyptic 180 million to 360 million." Yes, you read it correctly—180 to 360 *million*.

According to experts a virus today would move twice as fast as the earlier major flu outbreaks due to rapid means of travel. This quick spread of the virus would severely limit the ability of officials to halt its transmission with a vaccine. Even during the pandemic in 1968 that lasted 342 days, the flu moved more slowly.

The world is ripe for the kind of global scourge predicted in the Bible for the end times. Jesus forecasted sweeping plagues that would wreak havoc all over the world during the last days (Luke 21:11). The apostle John predicted that the fourth seal judgment, which will include plagues or pestilence along with other disasters, will wipe out 25 percent of the world's population. "Its rider was named Death, and his companion was the Grave. These two were given authority over one-fourth of the earth, to kill with the sword and famine and disease and wild animals" (Revelation 6:8).

No one can say for sure that any plagues or pandemics we currently see on the horizon are the ones predicted by Jesus or John. But we can say that globalism, rapid means of travel, and dense urban populations have paved the way for this kind of devastation to sweep the globe, leaving carnage in its wake.

FAMINE AND STARVATION

Another massive problem is starvation. Famine and starvation are caused by several factors: overpopulation, flawed domestic policies or institutional failure, and war. One of the obvious causes of famine in our world is overpopulation or overconcentration of people in certain areas.

Overpopulation is becoming a real problem, especially as people become more and more concentrated in urban settings. Consider the statistics on the exploding world population in the chart below:

World Population Growth

ESTIMATE	YEAR
1 billion	1804
2 billion	1927
3 billion	1959
4 billion	1974
5 billion	1986
6 billion	October 12, 1999

From 1900 to 2000 world population increased from 1.6 billion to 6.1 billion. World population in 2006 is estimated at about 6.6 billion.

Population growth in the United States and Western Europe has tended to slow in recent years, but in other portions of the world the population explosion continues. The world population increases at the dizzying rate of about eighty million people every year. Additionally, cities in urban areas gain about sixty million people every year. Social planners have warned that unless drastic changes are made in the birth rate, the need for food alone could cause a worldwide catastrophe in the next decade. It is only a matter of time before the number of people in the world exceeds the capacity of world food production and distribution. This will result in the starvation of millions of people.

The world food crisis greatly accelerated during the economic problems of the 1970s. In the 1980s the food crisis continued in various parts of the world, with millions of people dying of starvation. The energy problems of the Third World have contributed to the situation. The high cost of oil has reduced the supply of petroleum-based fertilizers and has made them too expensive for most underdeveloped countries. Droughts, storms, floods, and changes in climate have ravaged crops around the world as well.

Another real problem is that economic, structural, and political upheaval creates distribution problems so that even in places where crops normally would have been sufficient to feed the population, they were not available to meet people's needs. As natural disasters, civil war, and terrorism increase, the institutional structures to combat famine will be severely curtailed. Tensions will increase between the nations who have food and those that struggle with hunger. All the attendant ills of pestilence and disease present insuperable problems for the coming generation in underdeveloped countries.

CHRIST'S PROPHECY OF THE GREAT TRIBULATION

The Olivet discourse (Matthew 24–25) was Christ's answer to the disciples' question concerning the end of the age and described this same period. The Lord Jesus spared no words in describing the awfulness of the period. According to Matthew 24:15 (NIV), it will begin with "'the abomination that causes desolation,' spoken of through the prophet Daniel"; that is, the desecration of the Temple that Israel will build in the last days and the stopping of the renewed Jewish sacrifices and ceremonies. This will signal the beginning of the awful period.

Christ advised those in Judea at that time to flee to the mountains (Matthew 24:16). He advised them not to return to their houses to gather up anything, but to flee with utmost speed. It will be a time of great trial and trouble for those with small children. He instructed them to pray that their flight would not be in the winter, when the cold weather would make it more difficult, nor on the Sabbath, when Jews normally do not journey and their detection would be easier.

Christ concluded in Matthew 24:21-22 (NIV): "For then there will be great distress, unequaled from the beginning of the world until now—and never to be equaled again. If those days had not been cut short, no one would survive, but for the sake of the elect those days will be shortened." Here the same terminology is used as in Daniel 12:1, where the period is called "a time of distress such as has not happened from the beginning of nations until then" (NIV). Like Jeremiah and Daniel, Jesus calls that period unprecedented—there has never been a time like it in the history of the world, and there never will be another time like it.

Christ describes the days of tribulation as being so severe that if they were not "cut short," meaning "cut off" or "terminated," by His second coming, no one would survive the awfulness of the period, and all would perish. It is "for the sake of the elect" that Christ will come to terminate this period after three and a half years and deliver those who have put their trust in Him. By "the elect" He may have meant Israel as the chosen people, or both Jews and Gentiles who come to Christ in salvation during this awful period. They are the chosen ones, chosen for deliverance at the end of the period, and they will be delivered.

According to Romans 11:26: "And so all Israel will be saved. As the Scriptures say, 'The one who rescues will come from Jerusalem, and he will turn Israel away from ungodliness.'" Israel as a nation will be delivered from her persecutors, and although subject to searching judgment as described in Ezekiel 20:34-38, those who are judged worthy will enter into the blessedness of the millennial kingdom. Those survivors who will have turned to God during the Great Tribulation will become the parents and grandparents of new generations that will populate the earth during Christ's reign on earth. A similar judgment for Gentiles is described in Matthew 25:31-46, where the sheep are ushered into the Kingdom and the goats, representing the unsaved, are put to death. During the last three and a half years of the tribulation period, in spite of terrible disasters and persecution, God will miraculously provide for the survival of His people.

DETAILS IN THE BOOK OF REVELATION

The most detailed description of the Great Tribulation is found in the book of Revelation, beginning in chapter 6 and continuing throughout much of the book. In chapter 16 an unparalleled account is given of the terrible catastrophes and destruction of human life that will occur at the end of the period of chaos. The overall sequence of events in the period is described as the breaking of seven seals. As recorded in Revelation 4 and 5, in his vision of heaven John sees a scroll sealed on its edges with seven seals. When the scroll is unrolled, the first seal is broken, then the second, and in succession, all the seals through the seventh. These introduce events and situations that describe this general period.

In Revelation 6–19, there are seven seal judgments (Revelation 6–8), seven trumpet judgments (Revelation 8–9), and seven bowl judgments (Revelation 15–16). These series of judgments will be poured out successively during the Tribulation and will bring terrible disaster to everyone.

Seven Seals of Horror

The first seal portrays a terrible and satanic world government that will rule during the period of the Great Tribulation. This is described in more detail in Revelation 13. The second seal describes war, for the greatest war of all history will occur near the close of the period. The third describes famine, the result of both war and the catastrophes that will overtake the earth. The fourth seal describes death, for one-fourth of the world's population will be killed by war, hunger, disease, or wild animals.

Isn't it interesting that many of the new killer viruses that threaten to wipe out millions originate in animals or "the wild beasts of the earth"? A group of international scientists have concluded that the HIV virus that causes AIDS can be traced to African monkeys. The deadly Ebola virus, found in humans and primates, may be carried by fruit bats. The Nipah virus in Malaysia killed over one hundred people when it jumped from pigs to humans. So far, it has not jumped from human to human, but if it did, the death toll could be unimaginable. And the deadly bird flu that threatens a world pandemic comes from various kinds of birds. These may be the kinds of deadly diseases that wipe out billions.

The fifth seal reveals the extensive persecution of the period, for many who put their trust in Christ will seal their testimony with their own blood. The sixth seal describes the coming ecological nightmare. Stars will fall from heaven, and there will be disturbances in the seasons and cycles of nature. The sun will become black, and the moon will become as blood through the haze of destruction. Great earthquakes will move across the earth. Revelation 6 summarizes the entire period as a time when "the wrath of the Lamb" will be poured out on the earth—a time of divine judgment (Revelation 6:16).

Seven Seal Judgments

First Seal (Revelation 6:1-2)	White Horse: Antichrist
Second Seal (Revelation 6:3-4)	Red Horse: War
Third Seal (Revelation 6:5-6)	Black Horse: Famine
Fourth Seal (Revelation 6:7-8)	Pale Horse: Death and Hell
Fifth Seal (Revelation 6:9-11)	Martyrs in Heaven
Sixth Seal (Revelation 6:12-17)	Universal Upheaval and Devastation
Seventh Seal (Revelation 8:1-2)	The Seven Trumpets

Seven Trumpets of Disaster

The seven seals, however, are only the introduction—the general description of the period. When the apostle John sees the seventh seal on the scroll opened, the seven angels who stand before God are given seven trumpets that depict specific catastrophes, many of which will destroy large portions of the earth. Great disturbances will affect nature and change climates. A third part of the earth will be consumed by fire—either by a direct act of God or by God's use of other means, such as nuclear disaster or a disturbance of the earth's orbit around the sun. A third part of the sea will become as blood, and a third part of sea life will be destroyed. As the trumpets continue to sound, one catastrophe after another will afflict the earth. Demon possession will be common, as described in Revelation 9, and the torment of those afflicted with demons will be like the torment of one bitten by a scorpion.

The sixth trumpet signals the advance of a great army from Asia numbering two hundred million (Revelation 9:16). This will be a massive movement of men across the continent, probably led by China (see chapter 11). As startling as its size, so, too, will be its power to kill men. It will "kill one-third of all the people on earth" (Revelation 9:15). This apparently will be a human slaughter in addition to that mentioned in Revelation 6:8. The book of Revelation makes very clear that the combined catastrophes of this period will destroy more than half of the world's population.

Seven Last Bowls of Wrath

With the sounding of the seventh trumpet, a new series of catastrophes is revealed, as recorded in Revelation 16. These are the vials or

Seven Trumpet Judgments

First Trumpet (Revelation 8:7)	Bloody Hail and Fire: One-Third of Vegetation Destroyed
Second Trumpet (Revelation 8:8-9)	Fireball from Heaven: One-Third of Oceans Polluted
Third Trumpet (Revelation 8:10-11)	Falling Star: One-Third of Fresh Water Polluted
Fourth Trumpet (Revelation 8:12)	Darkness: One-Third of Sun, Moon, and Stars Darkened
Fifth Trumpet (Revelation 9:1-12)	Demonic Invasion: Possession and Torment
Sixth Trumpet (Revelation 9:13-21)	Two-Hundred-Million-Man Army: One-Third of Mankind Killed
Seventh Trumpet (Revelation 11:15-19)	The Kingdom: The Announcement of Christ's Reign

the bowls of the wrath of God. The symbolism is of a full bowl containing a judgment from God that will be poured out on the earth. As these successive bowls are poured out, great catastrophes will afflict the earth. Men's bodies will be covered with sores and afflicted with terrible pain; all life in the sea will die; the rivers and fountains of water will become as blood; unnatural heat will scorch the earth as the heavens are disturbed in their normal course. The sun will eventually be blackened, resulting in increasing darkness, changes in climate, and destruction of plant life.

The disasters poured out from the bowls of wrath are clearly described as the result of God's direct judgment. These judgments can be interpreted as supernatural acts of God, but some could also be interpreted as the consequences of a nuclear war that God allows. Nuclear war would cause tremendous loss of life, disturbance of the earth's orbit, and disruption of nature's cycles. The cumulative effects of nuclear war would cause human suffering from painful radiation burns and poisoning of water and food by radiation. Even a limited nuclear exchange could precipitate a series of earthquakes and geological activity that would continue a chain of destruction throughout the world.

Unusual demon activity will follow the pouring out of the sixth vial, which will dry up the Euphrates River and will further prepare the way for the great army from the East headed for Armageddon. The final judgment, described as the seventh bowl of the wrath of God, will occur during World War III, as the armies of the earth converge on the Middle East for the final desperate Battle of Armageddon. The entire earth will literally be shaken, its great cities will be destroyed, and the contour of the earth will be changed. Islands will disappear; mountains will be leveled.

This will be the final hour of divine judgment on a world that has rejected the Messiah and refused to let Christ reign over it. This war and series of plagues will leave a wake of almost unbelievable destruction of human life and property. It will be exactly what Christ

Seven Bowl Judgments

First Bowl (Revelation 16:2)	Upon the Earth: Sores on the Worshippers of the Antichrist
Second Bowl (Revelation 16:3)	Upon the Seas: Turned to Blood
Third Bowl (Revelation 16:4-7)	Upon the Fresh Water: Turned to Blood
Fourth Bowl (Revelation 16:8-9)	Upon the Sun: Intense, Scorching Heat
Fifth Bowl (Revelation 16:10-11)	Upon the Antichrist's Kingdom: Darkness and Pain
Sixth Bowl (Revelation 16:12-16)	Upon the River Euphrates: Preparation for Armageddon
Seventh Bowl (Revelation 16:17-21)	Upon the Air: Earthquakes and Hail

predicted—a time of trouble so great that if it were not terminated by His own second coming to the earth, no human life would survive. But this time of trouble will only be the background for God's final dealings with men. It will set the stage for the Battle of Armageddon and the judgments that will come when Jesus Christ returns.

See how today's headlines relate to this chapter at http://www.prophecyhotline.com.

THE LAST SUICIDAL BATTLE OF WORLD WAR III

EVENT #12: The armies of the world clash in the huge Valley of Meggido (Armageddon) in the final battle of World War III that begins just before the return of Jesus to planet earth.

> I turn back to your prophets in the Old Testament and the signs foretelling Armageddon, and I find myself wondering if we are the generation that is going to see that come about. I don't know if you have noted any of those prophecies lately, but, believe me, they describe the times we are going through.

PRESIDENT RONALD REAGAN (1983)

> There is no doubt that global events are preparing the way for the final war of history—the great Armageddon!

BILLY GRAHAM, *TILL ARMAGEDDON*

PEOPLE EVERYWHERE SEEM TO HAVE a sense that the world is moving rapidly toward some great crisis, possibly even a great finale. I'm sure you've felt this way yourself sometimes in light of all the danger, uncertainty, and instability the world faces. Statistics bear this out.

Here's a brief sample of what Americans believe about the book of Revelation and the end times.

> 59 percent believe that the prophecies in Revelation are going to come true.
>
> Nearly 25 percent believe that the Bible predicted the September 11 attack.
>
> 35 percent are paying more attention to how news events might relate to the end of the world.
>
> 17 percent believe the end of the world will happen in their lifetime.[1]

It seems clear that the collective sense of angst about our world and where it's headed is building. We all wonder how much longer until the lid blows off.

THE BLUEPRINT OF WORLD WAR III

Students of the Bible realize that prophecy provides a blueprint of the steps that will lead up to the final Great War, or what we might call World War III. It all begins with the rise of the final world ruler.

Proclamation of a New World Government

Ironically, the Antichrist will commence his world government by proclamation. Using his consolidated position of power in the Middle East, he will promise a new day of peace and prosperity for all who recognize his leadership. His message will be carried by television, radio, and Internet to the entire world in one day. The brilliant leader who enforced peace in the Middle East will seem to be the answer for a troubled world. His promise is a world government that will end all conflicts and bring plenty to the earth.

This man's absolute control of the world will give him power such as no man has ever had in human history. His brilliance as a leader will be superhuman, for he will be dominated and directed by Satan himself. But during his three-and-a-half-year rule, he will ruthlessly crush all opposition. His true character is indicated by the titles given to him in Scripture. He is described as "the beast" (Revelation 13:1-4), and Satan is described in his true character as "the great dragon" (Revelation 12:9; 13:4). This period of world history will be the culmination of Satan's dream to be like God, to control the world, to be the object of worship and adoration, and to secure the absolute obedience of all men.

The Rush to Judgment

The new world dictator's blasphemy, disregard of God, hatred of the people of God, and murder of countless believers in Christ will bring down the terrible divine judgments described in Revelation 6–18. Catastrophe after catastrophe will follow as the Great Tribulation unfolds.

The world will become increasingly discontented with the leadership of this world dictator who promised to bring them peace and plenty but instead brings the world one massive catastrophe after another. The wonders and miracles he will perform and his demands to be worshipped as God will only lead to the need for more oppression and persecution of dissenters. In spite of the tremendous power placed in the hands of the world dictator, he will be unable to control the situation. Major segments of the world will begin to rebel against him. Eventually they will converge in the Middle East to fight it out for international power.

The Outbreak of World War III

The prophet Daniel gave a graphic picture of this situation. After introducing the world ruler in Daniel 11:36-39 as an absolute ruler who will claim to be God, the prophet explained that the armies of the world will rise up in rebellion against him. According to Daniel 11:40, "Then at the time of the end, the king of the south will attack the king of the north. The king of the north will storm out with chariots, charioteers, and a vast navy. He will invade various lands and sweep through them like a flood."

Revolt from the South and North

Daniel's prophecy also described a great army from Africa, including not only Egypt but other countries of that continent. This army, probably numbering in the millions, will attack the Middle East from the south. At the same time Russia and the other armies to the north will mobilize another powerful military force to descend on the Holy Land and challenge the world dictator. Although Russia will have had a severe setback about four years earlier in the prophetic sequence of events, she apparently will have been able to recoup her losses enough to put another army in the field. The first battles of World War III will be confused as the armies move back and forth with varied success and failures. Apparently the world ruler will be able to crush some of the first attempts at revolt and gain some preliminary victories, especially in the south, and he will be able to drive back the invasion from Egypt and Africa.

China Makes Her Move

But even as the world dictator appears to gain control of the situation, a report will come of the advancing army from the east (Daniel 11:44). To contend with this advancing horde of two hundred million (Revelation 9:16), he will be forced to divert a major portion of his military strength to defend himself. Then further tidings will come of another army advancing from the north. At this point the greatest war of all history, involving hundreds of millions of people, will be set in motion, with the land of Israel as the major battleground. But this will be more than just another world war, for it will play a special role in preparing the world for the next series of prophetic events.

Satan's Battle Plan

According to Revelation 16:13-14, the armies of the world will gather by demonic influence. The world ruler, who was established and aided in his control of the entire world by the power of Satan, now will be attacked by armies that have been inspired to come to battle by demons sent forth from Satan.

In Revelation 16:13-14 (NIV), John writes: "Then I saw three evil spirits that looked like frogs; they came out of the mouth of the dragon, out of the mouth of the beast and out of the mouth of the false prophet. They are spirits of demons performing miraculous signs, and they go out to the kings of the whole world, to gather them for the battle on the great day of God Almighty." The unclean spirits, symbolized by frogs, represent demons who are Satan's messengers. They proceed out of the mouth of the dragon, the beast, and the false prophet—the evil trinity that is controlling the world.

The Satanic Trinity

Satan's program is always one of substitution. As Christians in their faith have a triune God—the Father, the Son, and the Holy Spirit—so the forces of evil will represent themselves as triune, with the dragon, or Satan, corresponding to God the Father; the beast corresponding to Christ as the King of kings and Lord of lords; and the false prophet corresponding to the Holy Spirit. Just as the task of the Holy Spirit is to cause all men to worship Christ and the Father, so the false prophet will cause men to worship the beast and the dragon. Proceeding from this evil trinity, the demons will go forth, supporting their work with satanic miracles. This demonic sorcery will deceive the kings of the earth into joining the world rebellion with the prospect of gaining world power.

The Battle of the Great Day of God

According to Scripture, the demons will "gather them for battle against the Lord on that great judgment day of God the Almighty" (Revelation 16:14, NIV). Why will Satan organize a world war to disrupt his world kingdom? Satan's desperate strategy will be much more important than his control of the world through the world dictator. Although from their point of view they are gathered to fight it out for world power, the armies of the world will actually be assembled by Satan in anticipation of the second coming of Christ. The entire armed might of the world will be assembled in the Middle East, ready to contend with the power of Christ as He returns from heaven. As subsequent events make clear, the movement will be completely futile and hopeless. The armies of the world are by no means equipped to fight the armies of heaven. Still Satan will assemble the nations for this final hour, and in fact, the nations will choose to side with Satan and oppose the second coming of Christ. It will be the best that Satan can do. These events will give the nations their choice and allow Satan his desperate bid to oppose Christ's second coming.

Armageddon

The world's armies will confront each other, gathered "to a place with the Hebrew name *Armageddon*" (Revelation 16:16). Armageddon is the Hebrew expression formed from the word *har*, meaning "mountain," and *Megiddo*, referring to a location in northern Israel. Mount Megiddo is a small mountain located near the Mediterranean Sea, overlooking a valley that stretches out to the east. This broad valley, some fourteen miles wide and twenty miles long, apparently will be the focal point for the marshaling of the armies for the final battle of World War III. Although much too small to contain the millions of men who will be involved, it will be the geographic focal point of the final world war and catastrophe popularly referred to as the Battle of Armageddon. Actually, the armies will be deployed for several hundred miles in every possible direction—north, south, and east.

As the armies of the world move toward the final Battle of Armageddon, the world war that has erupted will have already claimed millions of casualties. Scripture gives only a meager description of the major movements and battles involved. As the armies converge on the Valley of Armageddon, the world will be shaken by the last divine judgment of the series, described as the seventh bowl of wrath.

The apostle John explained the scene in these words:

And the demonic spirits gathered all the rulers and their armies to a place with the Hebrew name Armageddon. *Then the seventh angel poured out his bowl into the air. And a mighty shout came from the throne in the Temple, saying, "It is finished!" Then the thunder crashed and rolled, and lightning flashed. And a great earthquake struck—the worst since people were placed on the earth. The great city of Babylon split into three sections, and the cities of many nations fell into heaps of rubble. So God remembered all of Babylon's sins, and he made her drink the cup that was filled with the wine of his fierce wrath. And every island disappeared, and all the mountains were leveled. There was a terrible hailstorm, and hailstones weighing seventy-five pounds fell from the sky onto the people below. They cursed God because of the terrible plague of the hailstorm. (Revelation 16:16-21)*

To Curse God and Die

The armies of the world will be used as Satan's pawns for this final hour of victory. The revolt against the world dictator will cause the nations to assemble in the Middle East. The crescendo of wars and destruction will increase until the entire world is on the brink of oblivion. Rather than humble themselves, the leaders of the world will be ready to curse God and die (Revelation 16:9, 11, 21). The final showdown between God and the nations will be ready to occur.

The prophets revealed that all these events will be the preparation for the great climax of history in the second coming of Christ, the establishment of His Kingdom on earth, and the judgment of wicked men who would not have Christ reign over them.

The Rider on the White Horse:
From Manger to Power and Glory

In His first coming to earth, Jesus Christ was born in a stable, relatively unnoticed by the world. Announced by John the Baptist, He came as the servant and Savior described by the Old Testament prophets (Isaiah 42:1-4; 53:1-12). He lived in a time of comparative peace when the Roman Empire controlled Israel. He was tried and convicted in

177

Jerusalem. At the request of the Jewish leaders, He was nailed to a cross by Roman soldiers. Israel rejected the suffering Messiah who came as a servant. After His resurrection and appearance to many, He ascended into heaven from the Mount of Olives near Jerusalem.

The second coming of Jesus Christ to the earth will be no quiet manger scene. It will be the most dramatic and shattering event in the entire history of the universe. His coming in power and glory will seize the attention of the entire world. The revived Roman Empire will have expanded to a world empire with the world dictator's proclamation forty-two months earlier. After about three years the world empire will be torn by rebellion, resulting in a terrible world war, described in Daniel 11:40-45; Revelation 16:14-16; and Revelation 19:11-21. Millions of people will already have been killed in the previous fighting and disasters. Great armies from the north, south, and east will have reached the Middle East, with major contingents gathered in the Valley of Armageddon. Jerusalem, formerly a key city of the world dictator's rule, will be under attack, with house-to-house fighting (Zechariah 14:2). The entire world will then be stopped in awe by the final convulsive shaking of the earth (the last bowl of wrath, Revelation 16:17-21) and the dazzling appearance of the Son of Man descending from heaven with all His saints (Revelation 19:11-16).

In the New Testament the doctrine of the Second Coming is one of the major revelations of prophetic truth. It is estimated that one out of every twenty-five verses in the New Testament refers either to the Rapture of the church or Christ's second coming to set up His Kingdom. Christ Himself described His coming graphically as a glorious event, comparable to lightning coming out of the east and shining to the west (Matthew 24:27). He described His coming as the climax to the Tribulation:

Immediately after the anguish of those days, the sun will be darkened, the moon will give no light, the stars will fall from the sky, and the powers in the heavens will be shaken. And then at last, the sign that the Son of Man is coming will appear in the heavens, and there will be deep mourning among all the peoples of the earth. And they will see the Son of Man coming on the clouds of heaven with power and great glory. (Matthew 24:29-30)

Many other references to this event are found in the Gospels (Matthew 19:28; 23:39; Mark 13:24-37; Luke 12:35-48; 17:22-37; 18:8; 21:25-28).

Even on the occasion of Christ's departure from earth, the angels reaffirmed the doctrine of the Second Coming, addressing the disciples: "Men of Galilee, . . . why are you standing here staring into heaven? Jesus has been taken from you into heaven, but someday, he will return from heaven in the same way you saw him go!" (Acts 1:11). There are many other references to this event throughout the remainder of the New Testament (see Acts 15:16-18; Romans 11:25-27; 1 Corinthians 11:26; 2 Thessalonians 1:7-10; 2 Peter 3:3-4; Jude 1:14-15).

An Awesome Spectacle

The most detailed description of the Second Coming is found in the book of Revelation itself, which was named for the fact that Christ will reveal Himself to an awestruck world at His second coming. Revelation 1:7 states: "Look! He comes with the clouds of heaven. And everyone will see him—even those who pierced him. And all the nations of the world will mourn for him. Yes! Amen!"

The most graphic picture of all, however, is found in Revelation 19:11-21. As a climax to the Battle of Armageddon, the heavens will break open with the glory of God, fulfilling the prediction of Christ that His coming will be like the lightning shining from the east to the west. As revealed in other Scriptures, the heavens will have been darkened by earlier judgments from God (Matthew 24:29), but at that moment an unearthly, brilliant light will spread itself across the heavens, startling the entire earth.

As contending armies pause in their conflict, the heavens will open, and Christ will begin the majestic procession from heaven to earth. The words of this prophecy are the most dramatic to be found anywhere in world literature.

> *Then I saw heaven opened, and a white horse was standing there. Its rider was named Faithful and True, for he judges fairly and wages a righteous war. His eyes were like flames of fire, and on his head were many crowns. A name was written on him that no one understood except himself. He wore a robe dipped in blood, and his title was the Word of God. The armies of heaven, dressed in the finest of pure white linen, followed him on white horses. From his mouth came a sharp sword to strike down the nations. He will rule them with an iron rod. He will release the fierce wrath of God, the Almighty, like juice flowing from a winepress. On his robe at his thigh was written this title: King of all kings and Lord of all lords. (Revelation 19:11-16)*

This spectacle will certainly be an awesome one—millions of men and angels reflecting the glory of God and led by Christ astride a white horse, the symbol of a conqueror.

The world will first cringe in fear before this spectacle, but then the armies on both sides of the great world war will forget their differences and attempt to unite and fight the armies from heaven. This rebellion, inspired and organized by Satan (Revelation 16:13-14), will be a futile, suicidal effort to resist God. Revelation 19:15 describes the judgment that follows.

The sharp sword that goes out of the mouth of Christ is apparently a symbolic revelation of the command that will be issued. All the wicked hosts will be destroyed. The verses that follow reveal that the birds of the air will be invited to feast upon the flesh of the kings, mighty men, and horses slain in this great and catastrophic judgment (Revelation 19:17-18). The beast—that is, the world ruler—and the false prophet associated with him will be captured alive. According to Revelation 19:20, these two will be cast directly into a "fiery lake of burning sulfur."

The prophet Zechariah gives additional insight into the events related to the Battle of Armageddon. On the very day of the second coming of

Christ there will be house-to-house fighting in Jerusalem (Zechariah 14:2). The prophet also describes the dramatic geological upheaval that will occur when Christ finally sets foot on the Mount of Olives.

> *I will gather all the nations to fight against Jerusalem. The city will be taken, the houses looted, and the women raped. Half the population will be taken into captivity, and the rest will be left among the ruins of the city. Then the LORD will go out to fight against those nations, as he has fought in times past. On that day his feet will stand on the Mount of Olives, east of Jerusalem. And the Mount of Olives will split apart, making a wide valley running from east to west. Half the mountain will move toward the north and half toward the south. (Zechariah 14:2-4)*

The second coming of Christ will bring an abrupt halt to the final world war and the wave of destruction that will have almost destroyed the earth. His coming will also end the period of the Gentiles, during which Gentile nations determined the destiny of Jerusalem and oppressed the people of Israel.

CHRIST'S TRIUMPHANT RETURN

A complete understanding of the characteristics and background of Christ's second coming is crucial for every student of prophecy. The descriptions given in Scripture allow a sharp contrast to be made between Christ's second coming to earth and His earlier Rapture of the church. They allow us to make the following observations about His return. It will be:

A personal return. The second coming of Christ will be a personal return. The same Jesus Christ who was born of a virgin, who died on the cross, who rose again, and who ascended into heaven will soon come back bodily to the earthly sphere to exert His power and sovereignty in the world. It is quite clear that it will be a bodily return, not merely the spiritual presence of Christ. Zechariah 14:4 refers to the fact that "on that day his feet will stand on the Mount of Olives, east of Jerusalem." As the feet of Christ left the Mount of Olives in His ascension, so they will return, this time to demonstrate His omnipotent power.

A visible and glorious return. The return of Christ will be a visible and glorious return. According to Scripture, everyone will see Him (Matthew 24:30; Revelation 1:7). The second coming of Christ will not take place in a moment, as is true of the Rapture of the church. Christ's return will be a spectacular and majestic procession from heaven to earth that will take many hours. During this period, the movement of the procession and the earth's continued rotation will permit the entire world to witness the event. The ultimate destination of the procession will be to Israel, leading to the destruction of the armies assembled for the Battle of Armageddon and Christ's final descent to Mount Zion.

A return with the heavenly host. According to Scripture, a huge body of heavenly hosts, described as the armies of heaven, will accompany Christ in His second coming (Jude 1:14). Believers who were raptured at the beginning of the tribulation period, who are in heaven with the Lord as promised in John 14:1-4, will return to the earth as part of this vast company. Angels also will join Christ in this great procession from heaven to earth (Matthew 25:31).

A return that shakes the earth. After the armies of the world are already gathered for battle at Armageddon, the final bowl of wrath, described in Revelation 16:17-21, will be poured out, resulting in flashes of lightning, thunder, rumblings, and a severe earthquake. Cities will collapse, islands sink, and mountains disappear. Huge hailstones, each weighing seventy-five pounds, will fall from heaven. Then, after His procession from heaven and His destruction of the opposing armies, Christ's feet will touch the Mount of Olives outside Jerusalem. At that moment the mountain will be divided, and where the Mount of Olives stands today, a great valley will stretch out into the Jordan Valley below. This is only one of the tremendous changes that will take place in the topography of the Holy Land as a precursor to Christ's reign. Christ's second coming will drastically change the geography of the earth.

A return to judge the nations. In showing the majestic sovereignty of God in human history, the second Psalm gave this description of the world situation at the second coming of Christ: "The kings of the earth prepare for battle; the rulers plot together against the LORD and against his anointed one. 'Let us break their chains,' they cry, 'and free ourselves from slavery to God'" (Psalm 2:2-3).

The rebellion of the nations will draw a derisive laugh from the Lord. "But the one who rules in heaven laughs. The Lord scoffs at them. Then in anger he rebukes them, terrifying them with his fierce fury" (Psalm 2:4-5). Prophets throughout the Old Testament have pointed to a time when God will speak forth in righteous judgment on the earth. His final purpose is revealed in Psalm 2:6: "I have placed my chosen king on the throne in Jerusalem, on my holy mountain." At His second coming, Christ will claim possession of the nations as His inheritance. His judgments will be absolute, for as the psalmist predicted: "You will break them with an iron rod and smash them like clay pots" (Psalm 2:9). In light of this predicted judgment and the return of Christ, those who heard were instructed to serve the Lord and worship Him (Psalm 2:10-12). God promised to send His Son at the appointed time to reign over the earth and to begin His absolute rule of peace and justice. And so it will be that the rulers and their armies who resist Christ's return will be killed in a mass carnage. The rebels who are killed in the Battle of Armageddon will remain in their common grave until the final resurrection and judgment at the end of the thousand-year reign of Christ (Revelation 19:17-21).

A return to rule from Zion. The purpose of Christ's return to the Mount of Olives will be to establish Jerusalem as the capital of His new world kingdom. The law will once more go forth from Zion (Isaiah 2:3). Christ's return will save Jerusalem and the nation of Israel from complete annihilation. This direct intervention of God in saving Israel and returning Jews from all nations was predicted as early as the promise recorded in Deuteronomy 30:3: "Then the LORD your God will restore your fortunes. He will have mercy on you and gather you back from all the nations where he has scattered you."

Christ Coming to Judge and Rule

A multitude of Old Testament passages develop the same theme of a final kingdom of justice, righteousness, and peace to be established in Jerusalem. In Psalm 24 the gates of Jerusalem are urged to open and welcome the coming King. Psalm 72, in the form of a prayer, describes the reign of the coming King and the blessing and peace that will follow. In this final kingdom all kings will bow down before Him and the nations will serve Him (Psalm 72:11). Psalm 96 declares that His coming will be for judgment: "For he is coming! He is coming to judge the earth" (Psalm 96:13). Psalm 110 predicts that at the coming of Christ His enemies will be made His footstool, and He will reign in the midst of His enemies. It will be a time when Christ "will punish the nations and fill their lands with corpses; he will shatter heads over the whole earth" (Psalm 110:6).

The Major and Minor Prophets also address Christ's second coming. According to Isaiah 9:6, the child to be born will be the Mighty God and the Prince of Peace. When He comes, "His government and its peace will never end. He will rule with fairness and justice from the throne of his ancestor David for all eternity. The passionate commitment of the LORD of Heaven's Armies will make this happen!" (Isaiah 9:7). The entire eleventh chapter of Isaiah describes the coming of Christ and His judgment and righteous rule of the earth. Many other passages give a glowing description of the glorious kingdom of Christ on earth.

The Second Coming itself is pictured in Daniel 7:13-14: "As my vision continued that night, I saw someone like a son of man coming with the clouds of heaven. He approached the Ancient One and was led into his presence. He was given authority, honor, and sovereignty over all the nations of the world, so that people of every race and nation and language would obey him. His rule is eternal—it will never end. His kingdom will never be destroyed."

In a similar way Daniel 2:44 predicts that at His coming, Christ will establish His reign on the earth. "During the reigns of those kings, the God of heaven will set up a kingdom that will never be destroyed or conquered. It will crush all these kingdoms into nothingness, and it will stand forever."

Living Jews Regathered and Judged

The annihilation of the armies that resist Christ's return will be God's judgment on the nations. After the final carnage of the Battle of Armageddon, the surviving people of the world will be judged one by one. All living Jews, the surviving nation of Israel, will be brought home again, because God will leave none of His people behind (Ezekiel 39:28). Each one will face God as his judge, and none will escape this judgment. The rebels who have not accepted Christ as their Messiah prior to the Second Coming will be put to death (Ezekiel 20:38). The remaining believing Jews who have survived the persecution will be the first citizens of Christ's new Kingdom on earth. Their hour of persecution will be finished forever, and they will receive all the blessings that have been promised to the children of Israel since the time of Abraham (Jeremiah 31:31-34; Romans 11:26-27).

Other Survivors Face Judgment

The judgment of the non-Jews who survive the tribulation period is described in Matthew 25:31-46. According to this Scripture, Christ will gather all the Gentile population of the earth to appear before His newly established throne in Jerusalem. In this judgment, individuals will fall into one of two classes—the sheep or the goats. Christ as King will invite the sheep to enter into His Kingdom. They are the ones who will have aided the Jews during their intense persecution. They will have visited them in prison, clothed them when naked, fed them when hungry, and hidden them from their tormentors.

The greatest demonstration of true faith in God during this period of intense anti-Semitism will be action taken to help the suffering Jews. While these works in themselves will not be the basis of salvation, even in this period, to befriend a Jew during this time will be unmistakable evidence of true faith in Christ and an understanding of the Scriptures.

Accordingly, these believers will be known by their works in a difficult time, but like the believers of all ages, they will be saved solely by faith in God through the gracious death and redemption of Jesus Christ.

By contrast, unbelievers will be exposed by a revelation of their selfish cruelty toward the Jews during the Great Tribulation. These individuals, described as goats, will be cast into everlasting fire. Just as unbelieving Jews will be judged, so, too, unbelieving Gentiles will be judged.

The remaining population of the earth, still in their mortal bodies, will then enter the millennial kingdom of Christ's reign on earth. The Kingdom will begin with all unbelievers removed from the earth. As young children mature and new babies are born during the coming thousand-year reign, each of them will also have his or her moment to believe or rebel. But at the beginning of the period the rebels will have been completely purged, and the world will enter a new era of peace to rebuild and replenish the earth.

From Disaster to Utopia

A utopian world will follow the colossal failure of man's attempt to control human history. Three judgments will have purged the world of all who have not believed in Jesus Christ. The armies of the world will have been destroyed on the battlefields of the Middle East. Unbelieving Jews will have been judged and killed. In the judgment of the sheep and goats, unbelieving non-Jews will also have been purged from the earth. The entire adult population of the earth that remains will have experienced regeneration through faith in Christ.

Believers of the past will also have a part in Christ's reign of righteousness. The individuals who placed their faith in Christ during the centuries of the church age will be taken from the earth just before the end times begin. As explained in the next chapter, at the moment of the Rapture, the dead in Christ will be raised, and the living will be taken from the earth. In new, resurrected bodies they will join Christ in the heavens to be saved from the time of judgment on the earth. Believers who died during Old Testament times or during the time of Tribulation

Summary of Unfulfilled Prophecy

Rapture of the church	1 Corinthians 15:51-58; 1 Thessalonians 4:13-18
Revival of Roman Empire under ten leaders	Daniel 7:7, 24; Revelation 13:1; 17:3, 12-13
Rise of European dictator	Daniel 7:8; Revelation 13:1-8
Peace treaty with Israel signed seven years before second coming of Christ to establish His Kingdom on earth	Daniel 9:27
False world religion established	Revelation 17:1-15
Russia and her Islamic allies attack Israel about four years before second coming of Christ	Ezekiel 38–39
Peace treaty with Israel broken: world government, world economic system, world atheistic religion begins, three and a half years before second coming of Christ	Daniel 7:23; Revelation 13:5-8, 15-17; 17:16-17
Martyrdom of many Christians and Jews	Revelation 7:9-17; 13:15
Three crashing waves of catastrophic divine judgments poured out on the earth	Revelation 6–18
World war breaks out in Middle East: Battle of Armageddon	Daniel 11:40-45; Revelation 9:13-21; 16:12-16
Second coming of Christ	Matthew 24:27-31; Revelation 19:11-21
Judgment of the wicked	Ezekiel 20:33-38; Matthew 25:31-46; Jude 1:14-15; Revelation 19:15-21; 20:1-4
Satan bound	Revelation 20:1-3
Resurrection of Old Testament and Tribulation saints	Daniel 12:2; Revelation 20:4
Millennial kingdom begins	Revelation 20:5-6
Rebellion at end of the Millennium	Revelation 20:7-10
Resurrection and judgment of the wicked and Satan: Great White Throne Judgment	Revelation 20:11-15
Eternity begins: new heaven, new earth, new Jerusalem	Revelation 21–22

will be raised and given new, resurrected bodies at the time of Christ's second coming. This entire company of saints from the past will be present to observe and help administer the new Kingdom on earth.

In a dramatic turn of events, the King of kings and Lord of lords will have seized direct control of human history. A world formerly dominated by Satan and evil men will now be ruled in righteousness and equity. A world torn with war and disaster will enjoy a thousand years of peace. The surviving population of the earth will enter a golden age, when man's intelligence and best energies will be used to rebuild the world and live for the glory of God. Satan will be bound; evil will be directly and swiftly judged by God Himself. Nature will be released from bondage in this balanced and peaceful world where the lion will lie down with the calf (Isaiah 11:6).

THE QUESTION FOR THIS GENERATION

The series of crises in the Middle East during this generation is only the beginning of a series of events that will lead inevitably to the second coming of Christ. The first important series of prophetic events in our day came when Israel returned to her land and proved to the world that she would not be driven into the sea. The second series of prophetic events began when Europe and the world suddenly realized their common enemy in terrorism and their crippling dependence on Arab oil. Traditional power alignments have now been shaken, and a new coalition of European nations is emerging. As these events continue, the countdown to Armageddon could begin at any time. Our generation may well witness the stirring events described in the dramatic prophecies of the Old and New Testaments.

A pointed question is pertinent to each of us in this generation: Are we ready for the coming of the Lord?

See how today's headlines relate to this chapter at
http://www.prophecyhotline.com.

CHAPTER 14

A PROMISE TO REMEMBER

The Rapture: The act of Christ's raising up to heaven all living true believers.

Time, July 1, 2002

WHILE MANY DRAMATIC PROPHECIES AWAIT fulfillment at the end of the age, none is more important or heartwarming than a simple promise Christ made to His disciples. On the night before His crucifixion as He gathered with them in the upper room, Christ warned them that He was going to leave and that they could not follow Him. One of them was going to betray Him; another would deny Him. The disciples were deeply troubled.

In this tense atmosphere, Christ spoke the memorable words recorded in John 14:1-3: "Don't let your hearts be troubled. Trust in God, and trust also in me. There is more than enough room in my Father's home. If this were not so, would I have told you that I am going to prepare a place for you? When everything is ready, I will come and get you, so that you will always be with me where I am."

HOW THE NEW PROMISE DIFFERS
FROM THE SECOND COMING

This coming, often referred to as the Rapture of the church, was dramatically different from events Christ had announced in the Olivet discourse as recorded in Matthew 24. There He had predicted many events preceding His return to the earth. This will be a time of great tribulation, beginning with the desecration of the Jewish Temple and including a period of intense persecution for the people of Israel. This time of trouble will climax dramatically with the glorious appearing of Christ to set up His Kingdom.

But the promise Jesus made to the disciples in the upper room involved an entirely separate event—the coming of Christ to meet believers in the air, the Rapture of the church.

The promise of the Rapture added a new dimension to the disciples' expectations. Jesus was returning to heaven to prepare a place for them. He would return to receive them to Himself, taking them where He was in the Father's house. This was a promise of removal from earth and entrance into heaven. He mentioned no signs preceding and no tremendous prophecies that needed to be fulfilled before it happened. It was to be an imminent hope, an expectation each day after He left them.

Some Bible interpreters attempt to associate this coming of Christ for believers with His second coming to earth with the heavenly hosts from heaven to set up His kingdom (Revelation 19). But many other interpreters who have carefully studied this and other passages assert that Christ's coming for His own was predicted as an entirely separate event that will precede rather than follow other major end-time events.

Believers today can cling to the same hope that Christ promised His troubled disciples. It would be natural to be troubled if Scripture did not show that believers in this age won't face inevitable martyrdom in the Great Tribulation. Christians today need not fear the catastrophic days about to overcome the world. Instead, they have the imminent hope of Christ's return and their being joined to the Lord to enjoy His presence forever.

Years after the first announcement of this promise by Christ, the apostle Paul gave the Thessalonian church additional details on this precious hope, which he received through divine revelation (1 Thessalonians 4:13-18). He described this coming of Christ for His own as a truth that God wanted the Thessalonians to know and understand.

According to Acts 17:1-9, Paul, Silas, and Timothy preached the gospel in Thessalonica for three Sabbath days, with the result that "many God-fearing Greek men and quite a few prominent women" believed. But unbelieving Jews opposed Paul's ministry and threatened his life, so Paul and his companions left secretly by night to avoid being killed. Sometime later Paul sent Timothy back to see how the Thessalonians were getting along. Timothy's report to Paul gave a glowing testimony for Christ. Everyone in the region was talking about this Jesus of Nazareth who died and rose again to be the Savior of those who trusted in Him.

But Timothy also brought back theological questions that he could not answer, and one of them apparently related to the subject of the Lord's return. The Thessalonians believed that their loved ones who had died would be raised, but they wondered whether they would be raised before or after the coming of Christ for those still living. This question reveals that Paul had already taught them about the coming of the Lord for them. For these believers, the Rapture, the catching up of the church (1 Thessalonians 4:17), was an imminent hope, an event that would occur before the tremendous end-time judgments of God prophesied in the Old Testament. They simply wanted to know if their dead loved ones would be raptured with them.

In reply, Paul assured the Thessalonians that God did not want them to be ignorant about this truth or to sorrow like unbelievers who had no hope. He went on to assure them of the certainty of their hope in 1 Thessalonians 4:14: "For since we believe that Jesus died and was raised to life again, we also believe that when Jesus returns, God will bring back with him the believers who have died." This hope of Christ's return for the living and the dead was just as certain as were the facts of the death and resurrection of Christ, in which they had put their trust.

But what did Paul mean when he said that "God will bring back with him the believers who have died"? This is related to the truth found in 2 Corinthians that when Christians die their souls go immediately to heaven and we "would rather be away from these earthly bodies, for then we will be at home with the Lord" (2 Corinthians 5:8). Paul's answer to the Thessalonians was direct and easy to understand. When Christ comes from heaven to meet believers, He will bring these souls with Him. Their bodies will be raised from the grave at the Rapture, and their souls will reenter their resurrection bodies.

Paul then described the event:

> We tell you this directly from the Lord: We who are still living when the Lord returns will not meet him ahead of those who have died. For the Lord himself will come down from heaven with a commanding shout, with the voice of the archangel, and with the trumpet call of God. First, the Christians who have died will rise from their graves. Then, together with them, we who are still alive and remain on the earth will be caught up in the clouds to meet the Lord in the air. Then we will be with the Lord forever. (1 Thessalonians 4:15-17)

This new truth, not revealed in the Old Testament, was given to Paul "directly from the Lord" (1 Thessalonians 4:15). Those living at the time of the Lord's return will not go before the resurrection of the bodies of believers who have died.

Paul describes the scene this way: The Lord will descend from heaven with a shout, literally a shout of command. Christ will order the resurrection of the dead and the translation of the living.

This promise is in keeping with what Christ announced to His disciples while on earth when He said: "Don't be so surprised! Indeed, the time is coming when all the dead in their graves will hear the voice of God's Son, and they will rise again. Those who have done good will rise to experience eternal life, and those who have continued in evil will rise to experience judgment" (John 5:28-29).

Although the Rapture will be a partial fulfillment of His promise of the resurrection of the dead, since it involves only the resurrection of the Christians who have died in this age, it will be the Lord speaking with authority when He gives the shout of command. This will be accompanied by the voice of Michael the archangel (1 Thessalonians 4:16; Jude 1:9) and signaled "when the last trumpet is blown" or "the trumpet sounds" (1 Corinthians 15:52). It will be the final call for Christians, those who have heard the call of the gospel and responded in faith. They will have heard the call to service and yielded their hearts

A Comparison of the Rapture and the Return
(Christ's Second Coming)

THE RAPTURE	THE RETURN
Christ comes in the air (1 Thessalonians 4:16-17)	Christ comes to the earth (Zechariah 14:4)
Christ comes for his saints (1 Thessalonians 4:16-17)	Christ comes with his saints (1 Thessalonians 3:13; Jude 1:14)
Christ claims His bride	Christ comes with His bride
Not in the Old Testament (1 Corinthians 15:51)	Predicted often in the Old Testament
Imminent; no signs beforehand (1 Corinthians 15:52)	Many signs beforehand (Matthew 24:4-29)
A time of blessing and comfort (1 Thessalonians 4:18)	A time of destruction and judgment (2 Thessalonians 2:8-12)
Involves believers only (John 14:1-3; 1 Corinthians 15:51-55; 1 Thessalonians 4:13-18)	Involves Israel and the Gentile nations (Matthew 24:1–25:46)
Will occur in a moment; only Christ's own will see His advent (1 Corinthians 15:51-52)	Will be visible to the entire world (Matthew 24:27; Revelation 1:7)
Tribulation begins	Millennium begins
Christ comes as the bright morning star (Revelation 22:16)	Christ comes as the Sun of Righteousness (Malachi 4:2)

and lives to the Lord. This will be the end of their earthly pilgrimage and the beginning of eternity in the presence of the Lord.

A REUNION IN THE AIR

What a moment that will be! For the first time, believers in Christ will see the One whom, having not seen, they have loved (1 Peter 1:8). And what a reunion it will be for Christians who have been separated by death! Families will be reunited and friends will see each other again. Their joy at being in each other's presence will be increased by the fact that they will never be separated again. They shall be forever with the Lord.

In light of this marvelous promise, Paul tells the Thessalonians: "So encourage each other with these words" (1 Thessalonians 4:18). Such comfort would be impossible if believers first had to pass through the traumatic events of the Great Tribulation, which few would survive.

Some years later Paul added further light on this important subject when writing to the Corinthian church. After fourteen chapters of correcting them in various doctrinal and moral matters, in chapter 15 he set forth the great doctrines of the faith. He proclaimed again the gospel that Christ had died for their sins. The resurrection of Christ, he reasoned, is the basis for our hope for the resurrection of our own bodies from the dead. Our present bodies, which are destined for the grave, must necessarily be renewed and made over into heavenly bodies suited for spiritual experience and service in the presence of the Lord. Accordingly, in God's plan the normal course is birth, life, death, and resurrection for those who put their trust in Him.

At the close of the chapter, however, the apostle declared a mystery, a truth hidden in the Old Testament but revealed in the New Testament (Colossians 1:26). The new revelation was that there will be a grand exception to the normal rule of life, death, and resurrection. He declared: "But let me reveal to you a wonderful secret. We will not all die, but we will all be transformed! It will happen in a moment, in the blink of an eye, when the last trumpet is blown. For when the trumpet sounds, those who have died will be raised to live forever. And we who are living will also be transformed" (1 Corinthians 15:51-52).

Christians living on the earth at the time of the Lord's return will need to have their bodies transformed just as much as those who have died and been buried. As Paul pointed out, their bodies will be corruptible—subject to decay, age, and all the ills of this life. The bodies of Christians are mortal, that is, subject to death.

As Paul reasoned elsewhere (Ephesians 2:1-3; Philippians 3:21), men's bodies are also sinful, not suited for the holy presence of the Lord. A dramatic transformation is necessary, described here as a change to a body that will never grow old and will never die.

As Paul expressed it in 1 Corinthians 15:53: "For our dying bodies must be transformed into bodies that will never die; our mortal bodies must be transformed into immortal bodies." When this is accomplished at the time of the coming of Christ for His own, "Death is swallowed up in victory" (1 Corinthians 15:54).

THE RAPTURE MUST OCCUR BEFORE OTHER END-TIME EVENTS

By contrast, the many passages that deal with the second coming of Christ to set up His Kingdom never mention the translation of living saints, although they do describe the resurrection of martyred dead.

The reason is that saints who have lived through the horrific events will not be translated when Christ comes to set up His Kingdom but rather will be ushered into the millennial reign of Christ in their natural bodies. They will need to lead normal lives, plant crops, build houses, bear children, and repopulate the earth. Such would be impossible if all saints were translated and given heavenly bodies at the time of the introduction of the Kingdom. This is one important reason that the Rapture must take place earlier in the order of events before end-time troubles overtake the world.

Between the time when the church is caught up to heaven and Christ returns in triumph to set up His Kingdom, enough time must pass for a new body of believers, both Jews and Gentiles, to come to Christ and be saved. During the tribulation period of seven years, those living will have a final chance to believe and demonstrate their faith. Those who do will be the ones to populate the millennial earth. Those who have been translated and resurrected earlier at the Rapture will be in their resurrected, perfect bodies and will join Christ in His reign.

LIVING IN EXPECTATION

Paul assured the Corinthian church, just as he had the Thessalonians, of the wonderful hope of Christ's imminent return. Once again, he made no mention of any preceding events. As in other passages, the Day of the Lord, the age in which God deals directly with human sin, will begin immediately after the Rapture, as indicated in 1 Thessalonians 5. The fact that the Day of the Lord begins then makes clear that the church will not go through the judgments of the Day of the Lord and will not suffer the wrath of God, which will be poured out on unbelievers at that time (1 Thessalonians 5:9). These first-century Christians were challenged to live in expectation of Christ's coming, when the dead in Christ will be raised and living Christians translated. This blessed hope (Titus 2:13, NIV), this purifying hope (1 John 3:2-3, NIV), and this comforting hope (1 Thessalonians 4:18, NIV) should thrill the heart of every true believer in Christ. Especially in these momentous days, we should be alert to the challenge of being ready for the coming of the Lord.

 See how today's headlines relate to this chapter at
http://www.prophecyhotline.com.

SCANNING THE HORIZON

Now learn a lesson from the fig tree. When its branches
bud and its leaves begin to sprout, you know that summer
is near. In the same way, when you see all these things,
you can know his return is very near, right at the door.

JESUS CHRIST, MATTHEW 24:32-33

AS TODAY'S HEADLINES REPORT CURRENT developments in the
Middle East, serious students of prophecy expect the next dramatic
and important event to be the Rapture of all true believers. Skeptics
have been quick to point out that though the return of Christ has been
the hope of every generation since the time of the apostles, the promise has not been fulfilled. The apostle Paul clearly hoped that Jesus
would return in his lifetime and taught the early church to watch for
the Lord's return at any time. Likewise, the members of the early
church in Thessalonica believed that Christ might come in their lifetimes, and they were comforted by the expectation of being joined to

their deceased loved ones. But the centuries passed and the event has not taken place.

WHY HAS CHRIST DELAYED HIS COMING?

Why has Christ not already fulfilled His promise to come and receive His own unto Himself? From the human point of view, it may appear that Christ has delayed His return. Yet Scriptures make it plain that, from the divine standpoint, God is never late. In fact, when it comes to the fulfillment of biblical prophecy, delays are not unexpected. It has always been preceded by centuries of history that moved with sovereign precision to allow predicted events to occur exactly as promised, complete to the very last detail. For instance, Christ's first coming was also anticipated for thousands of years before it occurred, yet it took centuries for the earth to be prepared for His coming. During this time, the Greek language was developed and adopted throughout the Western world. This prepared the way for the New Testament to be written in a precise and widely used language.

Also, the Roman Empire was established and brought comparative peace in the Middle East. Jewish life and worship in Israel were ready for the Messiah's coming. John the Baptist came to announce the Messiah's coming and call the nation to repentance. The *Pax Romana* (the Peace of Rome) had opened international trade and communication, making it possible for first-century Christians to spread the gospel message throughout the entire Roman Empire and eventually the world.

The prophecies of Christ's first coming were fulfilled in a day carefully prepared by a sovereign God. The prophecies of Christ's return for believers and eventual second coming will be fulfilled in this way—in God's perfect timing.

But there is also a warm and personal reason why Christ has not returned. As the apostle Peter explains: "The Lord isn't really being slow about his promise, as some people think. No, he is being patient for your sake. He does not want anyone to be destroyed, but wants everyone to repent" (2 Peter 3:9). The delay of Christ's return to the earth for His own comes from a heart of love. A God of compassion is still waiting for many to hear the gospel and respond in belief. The delay is for us, so that we can respond in faith and carry this message to others.

The Scriptures indicate that God will not wait forever. Christ Himself used an illustration concerning His coming to establish His kingdom. He compared His coming to the times of Noah. When Noah built the ark in obedience to God's command, more than one hundred years elapsed before the Flood. Noah attempted to warn his generation, but they scoffed at his message and laughed at his efforts to build the ark. The day came, however, when the ark was finished and the animals went into the ark. Observers could have seen Noah and his family entering the ark. And then God shut the door (Matthew 24:37-39). Then it was too late! Those outside the ark perished in the flood that followed.

While Christ used this illustration in reference to His second coming, the same illustration can be applied to His coming for His church at the Rapture. God is patient and waits far beyond what human patience endures, but the time will eventually come when God will act.

Therefore, we have a special burden as well as a special privilege. Those who have confidently received Jesus Christ as Savior have the hope that they may at any moment be called to join Christ in the heavens. For those who have not responded in faith, the same moment will mark the beginning of a series of catastrophic events that will bring God's judgment on the world in which we live.

The burden of our generation is to make God's message of salvation clear in a time of confusion. Living faith brings happiness and meaning into our day-to-day existence. It also provides hope in a world that is rushing to judgment. Each of us must be sure that we have understood and responded to God's message of salvation.

The seriousness is that the time is short. Everyone must decide what they will do with Him. Jesus Christ was God who stepped out of eternity into time; was born of a virgin; lived a sinless life; and was rejected by His generation. He came to die on the cross for the sins of the world and rose the third day with a new resurrected body.

Christ ascended into heaven and will return to take those who believe in Him to Himself. All that is required of each and every one of us is that we accept His sacrifice by faith and invite Him into our lives. That begins a walk of faith that never ends. When He returns all those who have accepted Him as Savior will be taken out of this world. The Rapture is the first event in the unfolding of the end-time events described in this book.

Jesus died for you on the cross to purchase a pardon for your sins. All that God requires is for you to receive this pardon by faith and accept Christ as your personal Savior. "But to all who believed him and accepted him, he gave the right to become children of God" (John 1:12).

Once we understand this message we must lovingly communicate this urgent message to our families, friends, and everyone we can. The headlines are screaming that the time is short. The communication of this message is especially important in this generation that may witness the final hour of God's judgment on the world.

When the Rapture of the church was explained, no signs were ever given indicating the specific expectation of this event. Instead, believers in Christ were asked to look for His coming and to anticipate that it could occur at any time. This attitude characterized the early church and has been the hope of the church from the first century until now. But since there are no signs for the Rapture itself, what are the legitimate grounds for believing that the Rapture could be especially near for this generation?

The answer is not found in any prophetic events predicted before the Rapture but in understanding the events that will follow the Rapture. Just as history was prepared for Christ's first coming, in a similar way history is preparing for the events leading up to His second coming. Previous chapters in this book have explained the amazing historical developments that seem to be precursors to the predicted events that will occur soon after the Rapture.

THE THREE MAJOR DIVISIONS OF PROPHECY

Many different places, players, and events fill their own unique roles in the drama of the ages. This book has focused on twelve of these crucial events related to the end times.

To make it easier to grasp and discern where we are today in God's prophetic program, the major signs related to the end times are divided into three main categories: prophecies about the church, prophecies about the nations, and prophecies concerning Israel (1 Corinthians 10:32).

The prophecies that relate to the future of the church explain events and trends that will occur in the true church, as the body of believers, or in the organized church as an institution. Prophecies about the church as an institution often involve those who are only professing Christians. The Bible has much to say about this professing or organized church and the religious climate of the end of the age. These prophecies reveal the role of the superchurch and the False Prophet during the Tribulation period (Revelation 17:1-18) and the final rule of the Antichrist who will demand worship as God during the final years of the Tribulation.

The rise and fall of nations has been important to prophecies in both the Old and New Testaments. Of special interest today are prophecies that describe the international situation in the final years of history before Armageddon. These prophecies have a remarkable similarity to what we observe in the world today and, as such, constitute a warning of the approaching coming of the Lord.

Prophecies about Israel, and especially Jerusalem, provide important reference points for all of prophecy as well. The most significant prophetic event of the twentieth century was the restoration of the people of Israel to their land. All the prophecies of the end of the age indicate that at that time the Jews will be back in their land, precisely the situation in which they find themselves today.

Added to this situation is the worldwide expectation for a world government, which, according to Scriptures, will occur three and a half years before the Second Coming. Likewise, world religion, anticipated in Revelation 17, has already taken form in the world church movement which, after the Rapture, will be devoid of any true Christians.

These major situations that are true now, and that were not true seventy-five years ago, point to the conclusion that the Rapture itself may be very near. All areas of prophecy combine in the united testimony that history is preparing our generation for the end of the age.

In each area of prophecy a chronological checklist of important prophetic events can be compiled. In each list, in regard to the church, the nations, or Israel, the events of history clearly indicate that the world is poised and ready for the Rapture of the church and the beginning of the countdown to Armageddon.

A Prophetic Checklist for the Church

When all the predicted events relating to the church are placed in chronological order, it is evident that the world has already been carefully prepared for Christ's return. This checklist includes the major prophetic events in the order of their predicted fulfillment.

1. The rise of world communism made possible the worldwide spread of atheism.

2. Liberalism undermines the spiritual vitality of the church in Europe and eventually America.

3. The movement toward a superchurch begins with the ecumenical movement.

4. Apostasy and open denial of biblical truth are evident in the church.

5. Moral chaos becomes more and more evident because of the complete departure from Christian morality.

6. The sweep of spiritism, the occult, and belief in demons begins to prepare the world for Satan's final hour.

7. Jerusalem becomes a center of religious controversy for Arabs and Christians, while Jews of the world plan to make the city an active center for Judaism.

8. True believers will disappear from the earth to join Christ in heaven at the Rapture of the church.

9. The restraint of evil by the Holy Spirit will end.

10. The superchurch will combine major religions as a tool for the false prophet who aids the Antichrist's rise to world power.

11. The Antichrist will destroy the superchurch and demand worship as a deified world dictator.

12. Believers of this period will suffer intense persecution and be martyred by the thousands.

13. Christ will return to earth with Christians who have been in heaven during the Tribulation and end the rule of the nations at the Battle of Armageddon.

A Prophetic Checklist for the Nations

The prophetic events related to the nations can be compiled chronologically. Consider how the following list of significant world events—past, present, and future—shows that the world is being dramatically prepared for end-time events.

1. The establishment of the United Nations began a serious first step toward world government.

2. The rebuilding of Europe after World War II made a revival of the Roman Empire possible.

3. Israel was reestablished as a nation.

4. Russia rose to world power and became the ally of the Islamic world.

5. The Common Market and World Bank showed the need for some international regulation of the world economy.

6. China rose to world power and developed the capacity to field an army of two hundred million as predicted in prophecy.

7. The Middle East became the most significant trouble spot in the world.

8. The oil blackmail awakened the world to the new concentration of wealth and power in the Middle East.

9. The Iron Curtain fell, removing the final barrier to the revival of the Roman Empire.

10. The world clamors for peace because of the continued disruption caused by the high price of oil, terrorist incidents, and the confused military situation in the Middle East.

11. Ten leaders (the Group of Ten) will emerge from a European coalition—beginning the last stage of the prophetic fourth world empire.

12. In a dramatic power play, a new European leader will uproot three leaders of the coalition and take control of the powerful ten-leader group.

13. The new European leader will negotiate a "final" peace settlement in the Middle East (broken three and a half years later).

14. Russia and her Islamic allies will attempt an invasion of Israel but will be miraculously destroyed.

15. The European leader will proclaim himself world dictator, break his peace settlement with Israel, and declare himself to be God.

16. The new world dictator will desecrate the Temple in Jerusalem.

17. The terrible judgments of the Great Tribulation will be poured out on the nations of the world.

18. Worldwide rebellion will threaten the world dictator's rule as armies from throughout the world converge on the Middle East for World War III.

19. Christ will return to earth with His armies from heaven.

20. The armies of the world will unite to resist Christ's coming and will be destroyed in the Battle of Armageddon.

21. Christ will establish His millennial reign on earth, ending the period of the Gentiles.

A Prophetic Checklist for Israel

Although Israel's future cannot be separated from the wider sweep of history, prophecies about the Jewish people and the nation have their own distinct order of predicted events. In this prophetic checklist, as in the others, the events already in motion suggest the final countdown to Armageddon may already have begun.

1. The intense suffering and persecution of Jews throughout the world led to pressure for a national home in Israel.

2. Jews returned to the land, and Israel was reestablished as a nation in 1948.

3. The infant nation survived against overwhelming odds.

4. Russia emerged as an important enemy of Israel, but the United States came to the aid of Israel.

5. Israel's heroic survival and growing strength made it an established nation, recognized throughout the world.

6. Israel's military accomplishments were overshadowed by the Arabs' ability to wage a diplomatic war by controlling much of the world's oil reserves.

7. The Arab position is strengthened by their growing wealth and by alliances between Europe and key Arab countries.

8. The increasing isolation of the United States and Russia's growing alliance with nations in the Middle East make it more and more difficult for Israel to negotiate an acceptable peace settlement.

9. After a long struggle, Israel will be forced to accept a compromise peace guaranteed by the new leader of the European coalition.

10. The Jewish people will celebrate what appears to be a lasting and final peace settlement.

11. During three and a half years of peace, Judaism will be revived and traditional sacrifices and ceremonies be reinstituted in the rebuilt Temple in Jerusalem.

12. Russia and her Islamic allies will attempt to invade Israel but will be mysteriously destroyed.

13. The newly proclaimed world dictator will desecrate the Temple in Jerusalem and begin a period of intense persecution of Jews.

14. Many Jews will recognize the unfolding of prophetic events and declare their faith in Christ as the Messiah of Israel.

15. In the massacre of Jews and Christians who resist the world dictator, some witnesses will be divinely preserved to carry the gospel message throughout the world.

16. Christ will return to earth, welcomed by believing Jews as their Messiah and deliverer.

17. Christ's thousand-year reign on earth from the throne of David will finally fulfill the prophetic promises to the nations of Israel.

A COMPELLING SEQUENCE OF EVENTS

The earlier chapters of this book present the overall prophetic message about the future as it relates to history and today's headlines. Although prophecies about the church, the nations, and Israel are often presented in separate sections of biblical revelation, they are intricately related to each other in the unfolding of history. Israel obviously had to be reestablished as a nation in Palestine before many of these end-time events could begin. The coming leader of the European Union could hardly gain recognition by negotiation of a peace covenant with Israel if Israel did not exist or if there were no Middle East crisis. Without the economic necessity of oil and the fall of the Iron Curtain, European countries could hardly be expected to unite and take an active role in the Middle East crisis.

Many students of prophecy believe that Israel has now completed the first step in her restoration and fight for survival. Currently more Jews live in Israel than any other country in the world, yet they still do not live in peace with their neighbors. The Bible predicts that lasting peace will not come in the Middle East until a new world leader emerges from the Group of Ten leaders who begin the revival of the Roman Empire.

The signing of that peace settlement is the second step in Israel's prophetic calendar, and it will mark the beginning of the last seven years before Armageddon. These last seven years will be a time when evil is unrestrained and God's judgment is poured out on the world. The third step in Israel's restoration will begin when her peace treaty is broken. The fourth and final step will begin with the return of Christ and Israel's deliverance.

For those who believe in Christ, Israel's present situation is tremendously significant. If the next stage in Israel's restoration cannot come until the church is removed, the coming of Christ for His followers must occur soon. As the Middle East crisis continues, powerful alliances will emerge between European and Arab countries. But the coming world dictator cannot make his decisive move until the church is removed. Only then will Satan have a free hand to manipulate history using the forces of evil. For these reasons, informed Christians expect that the coming of the Lord is the next important event on the prophetic calendar.

THE FINAL STAGE IS SET

The world today is like a stage being set for a great drama. The major actors are already in the wings waiting for their moment in history. The main stage props are already in place. The prophetic play could begin at any time. The Middle East now occupies the attention of the world leaders. Those who control the tremendous oil reserves of the area have great political and economic power. The meteoric rise of Islamic fundamentalism, the election of Hamas to power in Palestine, the presence of Hezbollah in Lebanon, and Iran's determination to destroy Israel have lit the fuse to an already explosive situation. Israel desperately needs the covenant of peace promised in prophecy. Old friendships may change as European nations seek new alliances and agreements to protect themselves in a changing world situation. The Middle East will continue to be the focal point of international relationships.

Russia is poised to the north of the Holy Land for entry in the end-time conflict. China is now a military power great enough to field an army as large as that described in the book of Revelation. Each nation is ready to play out its role in the final hours of history.

Our present world is well prepared for the beginning of the prophetic drama that will lead to Armageddon. Since the stage is set for this dramatic climax of the age, it must mean that Christ's coming for His own is very near. If there ever was an hour when men should consider their personal relationship to Jesus Christ, it is today. God is saying to this generation: "Prepare for the coming of the Lord."

See how today's headlines relate to this chapter at
http://www.prophecyhotline.com.

Acknowledgments

THIS BOOK BECAME A PROJECT with a life of its own—through the vision and dedicated work of many people. If my father were still alive, I know he would affirm everything in the book. It faithfully represents his vision and understanding of what the Scriptures teach about the future. Many hearts and minds joined together to make this happen.

Before my father died he confirmed the outline of prophecy that had been his life's work. He asked me to put together a revised and expanded edition of *Armageddon, Oil and the Middle East Crisis*. He suggested the title *Armageddon, Oil, and Terror* and outlined the strategy and concepts presented in this work. Although I had written the previous editions of the book with his guidance, I realized I needed someone with special knowledge and talent to help fulfill my father's larger vision for this new work.

A total stranger called me a couple of years after my father's death and asked the question, "It's been fourteen years since the last edition of *Armageddon*; isn't it time to publish it again with everything that is happening in the world?" The caller, an author and avid student of prophecy, then went on to explain how events unfolding in the news were exactly what my father outlined in the previous editions of the book.

The caller, Dr. Mark Hitchcock, had already authored more than a dozen books on Bible prophecy. He had known and admired my father. They became friends when Mark was a student at Dallas Theological Seminary. His study of the Scriptures confirmed every detail of biblical prophecy my father had taught.

I asked Dr. Hitchcock to work with me as writer and researcher for this edition. We worked as a team for more than two years to complete this book. In the process I discovered Dr. Hitchcock to be a wise and godly man who understands what the Scriptures teach about the future. We spent many hours discussing the key points in the book—and always arrived at the same conclusions. His contribution to this edition and to my father's legacy has been immense. He has been like a brother to me in this project.

As the manuscript was being completed, John Van Diest became a champion for the book. John is a friend and had studied under my father. He understood exactly why this book had to be published. His excitement and passion were contagious.

Doug Knox, at Tyndale House Publishers, embraced our vision and helped us put together an amazing team to publish this book. Jan Long Harris joined in to shape the direction of the book. I have greatly appreciated her friendship, gracious spirit, and thorough oversight as she led the team inside Tyndale.

Kim Miller became much more than our editor. She took the time to familiarize herself with the complexities of end-time prophecy. Many of her suggestions and insights were incorporated into the book. Mark Hitchcock and I both believe the book was greatly enhanced by her remarkable editorial work.

Many others at Tyndale have contributed to the launch of this book. Their dedication and vision helped take this important book to a new generation of readers.

But most of all, I appreciated the support and understanding of Mark Taylor, president of Tyndale House Publishers. His father, Ken Taylor, and my father were friends during their lifetime. Mark instantly understood what I was trying to accomplish with the book. He understands what it means to secure a father's legacy. His leadership has secured his father's legacy and has made Tyndale the amazing publisher it is today.

My thanks to everyone on the team.

—John E. Walvoord

I AM DEEPLY GRATEFUL FOR the opportunity John gave me to be part of this project. I loved his father, learned a great deal from him, and held him in highest esteem. Working on this book has been one of the major highlights of my life and ministry. One of the unexpected blessings to come out of this project is that John and I have developed a friendship that I will always treasure.

—Mark Hitchcock

Endnotes

Preface

1. John F. Walvoord, "Is the Seventieth Week of Daniel Future?" *Bibliotheca Sacra* 101 (January–March 1944), 30–49; "Is the Church the Israel of God?" *Bibliotheca Sacra* 101 (October–December 1944), 403–416; "The Fulfillment of the Abrahamic Covenant," *Bibliotheca Sacra* 102 (January–March 1945), 27–36; "The Fulfillment of the Davidic Covenant," *Bibliotheca Sacra* 102 (April–June 1945), 153–166; "Israel's Blindness," *Bibliotheca Sacra* 102 (July–September 1945), 280–290; "Israel's Restoration," *Bibliotheca Sacra* 102 (October–December 1945), 405–416.

CHAPTER 1
Why Prophecy?

1. Strategic Issues Research Institute, *Strategic Issues Today*, 18 October 2001.
2. "2 Hurt by Saudi Bomb Die," *New York Times*, 26 February 2006.
3. Michael Hirsh, Melinda Liu, and George Wehrfritz, "We Are a Nuclear Power," *Newsweek*, 23 October 2006, 36.

CHAPTER 2
Oil Becomes the Ultimate Weapon

1. PBS, "Charting the World's Oil," see http://www.pbs.org/frontlineworld/stories/colombia/images/map.swf. See also Robert Samuelson, "An Oil Habit America Cannot Break," *Washington Post*, 18 October 2006, A21.
2. Tim Appenzeller, "The End of Cheap Oil," *National Geographic*, June 2004, 88. For another intriguing analysis of this situation, see Matthew Simmons, "Shock to the System: The Impending Global Energy Supply Crisis," *Harvard International Review* (Fall 2006).
3. Peter Tertzakian, *A Thousand Barrels a Second* (New York: McGraw-Hill, 2006), 3.
4. Appenzeller, "The End of Cheap Oil," 88.
5. Ibid., 90.
6. Adam Lashinsky and Nelson D. Schwartz, "How to Beat the High Cost of Gasoline. Forever!" *Fortune*, 6 February 2006, 74, 80.

7. Energy Information Administration, *Monthly Energy Review*, July 2006, table 1.7.

8. Paul Tharp, "Oil Prices Pump Up ExxonMobil Profits," *New York Post*, 27 October 2006; http://www.nypost.com/seven/10272006/business/oil_prices_pump_up_exxonmobil_profits_business_paul_tharp.htm (accessed December 12, 2006).

9. Peter Huber and Mark Mills, "Getting Over Oil," *Digital Power Group Commentary*, September 2005, http://www.digitalpowergroup.com/downloads/Commentary-Sept05.htm (accessed December 14, 2006). See also "American-Made Energy Freedom Act," http://www.house.gov/nunes/documents/AMEF_TP.pdf (accessed December 14, 2006).

10. Lashinsky and Schwartz, "How to Beat the High Cost of Gasoline," 74.

11. Ibid., 87.

12. David Pimentel, "Limits of Biomass Utilization," *Encyclopedia of Physical Sciences and Technology* (Academic Press, 2001); findings cited at http://www.healthandenergy.com/ethanol.htm (accessed December 12, 2006). To read the U.S. Department of Energy's rebuttal to some of his claims, see http://www.eere.energy.gov/afdc/altfuel/eth_energy_bal.html.

13. Adam Wilmoth, "Is Ethanol Sector Growing Too Fast?" *Daily Oklahoman*, 5 January 2007.

14. Nathanael Greene and Yerina Mugica, "Bringing Biofuels to the Pump," issue paper from the Natural Resources Defense Council, July 2005, 2.

15. Lashinsky and Schwartz, "How to Beat the High Cost of Gasoline," 75.

16. Ibid.

17. Council on Foreign Relations, *National Security Consequences of U.S. Oil Dependency*, Independent Task Force Report No. 58, released October 12, 2006.

18. Paul Roberts, *The End of Oil* (New York: Mariner Books, 2005), 337.

CHAPTER 3
Terrorism Reaches Everyone

1. William J. Broad and David E. Sanger, "New Worry Rises on Iranian Claim of Nuclear Steps," *New York Times*, 17 April 2006. See also Carnegie Endowment for International Peace, *A. Q. Khan Nuclear Chronology*, Issue Brief 8, no. 8, September 7, 2005, see http://www.carnegieendowment.org/static/npp/Khan_Chronology.pdf (accessed December 12, 2006). See also Kenneth R. Timmerman, *Countdown to Crisis: The Coming Nuclear Showdown with Iran*, updated ed. (2005; repr., New York: Three Rivers Press, 2006), 263–264.

2. The Nuclear Threat Initiative provides a summary of Iran's nuclear capabilities at http://www.nti.org/e_research/profiles/Iran/1825_6279.html.

3. Rown Scarborough, "U.S. Military Sees Iran's Nuke Bomb 5 Years Away," *Washington Times*, 31 August 2006.

4. The Lugar Letter, July 2005; see http://www.lugar.senate.gov/newsletter/2005/july.html (accessed December 12, 2006).

5. CBS News, "Experts Warn of Future WMD Attack," June 22, 2005, http://www.cbsnews.com/stories/2005/06/22/world/main703465.shtml?CMP=ILC-SearchStories (accessed December 12, 2006).

CHAPTER 4
Israel: Ground Zero for the End Times

1. Thomas Ice and Timothy Demy, *The Truth about Jerusalem in Bible Prophecy* (Eugene, Ore.: Harvest House Publishers, 1996), 8.

2. Clarence Larkin, an American pastor, introduced this concept in the early twentieth century in his book *Dispensational Truth (or God's Plan or Purpose in the Ages)*.

CHAPTER 5

The Decline and Fall of America

1. Peter Tertzakian, *A Thousand Barrels a Second* (New York: McGraw-Hill, 2006), xii–xiii.
2. According to a 2002 ABC News/BeliefNet Poll, 83 percent of Americans identify themselves as Christians. Another 13 percent say they have no religion. Just 4 percent describe themselves as Jewish, Muslim, Buddhist, or another religion. That compares to only 33 percent of the world at large who identify themselves as Christians. See a summary of this poll at http://abcnews.go.com/sections/us/ DailyNews/beliefnet_poll_010718.html (accessed December 14, 2006). See also Patrick Johnstone, *Operation World,* 4th Edition (Grand Rapids, Mich.: Zondervan, 1987), 34.

CHAPTER 6

The New *Pax Romana*

1. Michael T. Klare, *Blood and Oil* (New York: Henry Holt and Company, 2004), 146.

CHAPTER 7

The Russian–Islamic Invasion of Israel

1. For more on the Ezekiel 38–39 prophecy, with special focus on the role of modern-day Iran, see Mark Hitchcock's book *Iran: The Coming Crisis* (Sisters, Ore.: Multnomah, 2006), 160–166.
2. Josephus, *Antiquities of the Jews* 1.6.1.
3. C. F. Keil, *Ezekiel, Daniel, Commentary on the Old Testament,* trans. James Martin (Grand Rapids: Eerdmans Publishing Company, 1982), 159. Wilhelm Gesenius, *Gesenius' Hebrew-Chaldee Lexicon to the Old Testament Scriptures* (Grand Rapids: Eerdmans Publishing Company, 1949), 752.
4. Clyde E. Billington Jr., "The Rosh People in History and Prophecy, Part 2," *Michigan Theological Journal* 3 (1992): 54–61.
5. G. A. Cooke, *A Critical and Exegetical Commentary on the Book of Ezekiel,* ICC, ed. S. R. Driver, A. Plummer, and C. A. Briggs (Edinburgh: T. & T. Clark, 1936), 408–9. John Taylor agrees. He says, "If a place-name *Rosh* could be vouched for, RV's *prince of Rosh, Meshech, and Tubal* would be the best translation." See John B. Taylor, *Ezekiel: An Introduction & Commentary,* Tyndale Old Testament Commentaries, gen. ed. D. J. Wiseman (Downers Grove, Ill.: InterVarsity Press, 1969), 244. Since it appears that there was a place in Ezekiel's day known as Rosh, this is the superior translation. For an extensive, thorough presentation of the grammatical and philological support for taking Rosh as a place name, see James D. Price, "Rosh: An Ancient Land Known to Ezekiel," *Grace Theological Journal* 6 (1985): 67–89.
6. Gesenius died in 1842. See *Gesenius' Hebrew-Chaldee Lexicon.*
7. Clyde E. Billington Jr. "The Rosh People in History and Prophecy, Part 2)," *Michigan Theological Journal* 3 (1992): 145–46; Billington, "The Rosh People in History and Prophecy, Part 3)," *Michigan Theological Journal* 4 (1993): 59, 61; James D. Price, "Rosh: An Ancient People Known to Ezekiel," *Grace Theological Journal* 6 (1985): 71–73; Jon Mark Ruthven, *The Prophecy That Is Shaping History* (Fairfax, Va.: Xulon Press, 2003).
8. Josephus, *Antiquities* 1.6.1.
9. Adrian Blomfield, "Putin Is Returning Russia to a State of Tyranny," November 22, 2006, telegraph.co.uk, http://www.telegraph.co.uk/opinion/main.jhtml?xml=/opinion/2006/11/22/do2205.xml (accessed December 13, 2006). Ethan S. Burger, "The Price of Russia's 'Dictatorship of Law,'" *Christian Science Monitor,* 12 October 2006. Political scientist Arnold Beichman has dubbed Putin "Stalin lite."
10. "Putin Deplores Collapse of USSR," BBC News, April 25, 2005, http://news.bbc.co.uk/2/hi/europe/4480745 .stm (accessed December 13, 2006).

11. You can find additional details on Ahmadinejad's background and beliefs in Mark Hitchcock's book *Iran: The Coming Crisis* (Sisters, Ore.: Multnomah, 2006), 68–80.

12. Kenneth R. Timmerman, *Countdown to Crisis: The Coming Nuclear Showdown with Iran*, updated ed. (2005; repr., New York: Three Rivers Press, 2006), 331.

13. The first and third statements were reported in Ali Akbar Dareini, "Iran Hits Milestone in Nuclear Technology," Associated Press, 11 April 2006. PBS's *NewsHour* reported the second in its segment "Iran Nuclear Program Defies UN," which aired on April 11, 2006, http://www.pbs.org/newshour/bb/middle_east/jan-june06/iran_4-11.html (accessed December 14, 2006).

14. The Press Association, "Iran President: Wipe Israel Off Map," October 27, 2005, http://news.scotsman.com/latest.cfm?id=2152412005 (accessed December 13, 2006).

15. The Anti-Defamation League has compiled an extensive list of Ahmadinejad statements. See http://www.adl.org/main_Anti_Semitism_International/ahmadinejad_words.htm.

16. Ibid.

17. Agence France-Presse, "Iran Increases Palestinian Aid to 120 Million Dollars," http://www.iranpress-news.com/english/source/017682.html (accessed December 13, 2006).

18. Yaakov Lappin, "Iranian Paper: Great War to Wipe Out Israel Coming, *Ynetnews*, 15 November 2006, http://www.ynetnews.com/articles/0,2340,L-3328416,00.html (accessed December 13, 2006).

19. Ibid.

20. The Middle East Media Research Institute, "Iran President Ahmadinejad: 'I Have a Connection with God . . . ,'" Special Dispatch Series—No. 1328, 19 October 2006, http://memri.org/bin/articles.cgi? Page=archives&Area=sd&ID=SP132806 (accessed December 13, 2006).

21. Anton La Guardia, "'Divine Mission' Driving Iran's New Leader," telegraph.co.uk, 14 January 2006, http://www.telegraph.co.uk/news/main.jhtml?xml=/news/2006/01/14/wiran14.xml&sSheet=/news/2006/01/14/ixworld.html (accessed December 13, 2006).

22. Ellen Knickmeyer and K. I. Ibrahim, "Bombing Shatters Mosque in Iraq," *Washington Post*, 23 February 2006, http://www.washingtonpost.com/wp-dyn/content/article/2006/02/22/AR2006022200454.html (accessed December 14, 2006).

23. Timmerman, *Countdown to Crisis*, 325.

24. Ibid., 326–327.

25. Arnaud de Borchgrave, "The Apocalyptic Vision of Iranian President Ahmadinejad," NewsMax.com, 9 February 2006, http://www.newsmax.com/archives/articles/2006/2/8/154740.shtml (accessed December 13, 2006).

26. Ibid.

27. Daniel Pipes, "The Mystical Menace of Mahmoud Ahmadinejad," *New York Sun*, 10 January 2006, http://www.danielpipes.org/article/3258 (accessed December 13, 2006).

28. La Guardia, "'Divine Mission' Driving Iran's New Leader."

29. Mortimer B. Zuckerman, "Moscow's Mad Gamble," *U.S. News & World Report*, 30 January 2006, 1.

30. *Enhanced Global Intelligence Brief*, September 30, 2005.

31. Gerard Baker, "Let's Not Talk Turkey: Guess Who Won't Be Joining the European Union Anytime Soon," *The Weekly Standard*, 29 August 2005.

CHAPTER 8

The Coming World Dictator: "The World Is Mine, and I Am God"

1. See http://www.freedomdomain.com/nwoquote.htm.

2. Harold H. Hoehner, *Chronological Aspects of the Life of Christ* (Grand Rapids, Mich.: Zondervan, 1977), 115–140. The chart on page 122 is adapted from page 139 of this book.

CHAPTER 9

The Final Holocaust

1. CNN.com, "Iranian Leader: Holocaust a Myth," 14 December 2005, http://www.cnn.com/2005/WORLD/ meast/12/14/iran.israel (accessed December 13, 2006).
2. Nazila Fathi, "Israel Fading, Iran's Leader Tells Deniers of Holocaust," *New York Times*, 13 December 2006.
3. For more on this, see Mark Hitchcock, *What On Earth Is Going On?* (Sisters, Ore.: Multnomah, 2002), 55–57.

CHAPTER 10

Iraq: The New Babylon—Economic Center of World Power

1. I explore Iraq and its relationship to the end times in greater detail in my book *Seven Signs of the End Times* (Sisters, Ore.: Multnomah, 2003).
2. Barbara Slavin, "Giant U.S. Embassy Rising in Baghdad," *USA Today*, 19 April 2006.
3. Bay Fang, "An Oil Rush in (Yes) Iraq," *U.S. News & World Report*, 13 November 2006, 56.
4. Ibid.
5. Ibid.

CHAPTER 11

China Flexes Its Awesome Power

1. Richard J. Newman, "The Rise of a New Power," *U.S. News & World Report*, 20 June 2005, 40.
2. Michael Elliott, "The Chinese Century," *Time*, 22 January 2007, 32–41.
3. U.S. Department of Defense, *Quadrennial Defense Review Report*, (Washington, D.C.: February 6, 2006), 9.
4. Bibhudatta Pradhan and Anand Krishnamoorthy, "China, India to Boost Trade, Investment, Energy Ties," Bloomberg.com, 21 November 2006, http://www.bloomberg.com/apps/news?pid=20601102&sid=aFB _NIbsDUOA&refer=uk (accessed December 14, 2006).
5. Newman, "The Rise of a New Power."
6. Stephen Leeb, "A More Cautious Way to Play Energy and Chindia," *The Complete Investor* 4, no. 1 (January 2006), 2.
7. Matthew Forney, "China's Quest for Oil," *Time*, 18 October 2004.
8. U.S. Central Intelligence Agency, *The World Factbook* (Washington, D.C.: 2006). China's total manpower available for military service is estimated at 343 million (males aged 18–49), but the military manpower fit for military service (ages 18–49) is 281,240,272. This number is rising at a rate of about 13 million per year.

CHAPTER 12

Natural Disasters, Disease, and Famine Reach Everyone

1. Charles Krauthammer, "Flu Hope, or Horror?" *Washington Post*, 14 October 2005.
2. Tim Appenzeller, "Tracking the Next Killer Flu," *National Geographic* 208, no. 4 (October 2005): 2–31.

CHAPTER 13

The Last Suicidal Battle of World War III

1. Nancy Gibbs, "Apocalypse Now," *Time*, 1 July 2002, 42–48.

John F. Walvoord
The Father of Modern Biblical Prophecy

NO SINGLE INTELLECTUAL VOICE CONTRIBUTED more to the development of modern biblical prophecy than Dr. John F. Walvoord. During his six-decade-long career as an author, pastor, teacher, and educator, Dr. Walvoord articulated a comprehensive view of biblical prophecy that was based on his rock-solid belief that all the prophecies in the Bible either have been, or will be, literally fulfilled.

Dr. Walvoord began his teaching career as a professor of theology at Dallas Theological Seminary in 1936. In 1952, after the death of Dr. Lewis Sperry Chafer, the seminary's founder and first president, Dr. Walvoord became president and built it into a formidable graduate school of theology. In 1986, after serving Dallas Theological Seminary for fifty years, Dr. Walvoord became chancellor.

From the beginning of his professional career, Dr. Walvoord spoke and wrote about biblical prophecy in light of current world events. Even before the world believed there could be a Jewish return to the Holy Land or a nation of Israel, Dr. Walvoord insisted that a new Jewish state would emerge and that no one, whether it be the British, the Palestinians, or the Arab nations, could stop this inevitable fulfillment of biblical prophecy.

Before the Arab-Israeli wars of the 1960s, Dr. Walvoord maintained that Israel would win more land and power. He saw God's plan for the end times begin to unfold as the Palestinian-Israeli conflict became the focus of NATO and Western leaders. He taught that soon all the nations of the world would be embroiled in conflict leading to the events prophesied in the books of Daniel and Revelation.

Walvoord's studies led him to author, coauthor, or edit more than fifty books on Bible prophecy. One, *Armageddon, Oil and the Middle East Crisis,* became an international best seller in 1974. This work was later revised and expanded in 1990 during the Gulf War with Iraq. More than two million copies of this work are in print, and it has been translated into ten languages. This work proved the value of biblical prophecy in explaining world events.

Dr. Walvoord believed that the events of September 11, 2001, were the opening salvo to acts of sacred terror in the name of jihad that would push the world to the brink of destruction. In addition, he sensed that weapons of mass destruction would proliferate and force the West into preemptive military strikes. The need for oil would require massive military intervention to protect the oil fields of the Middle East.

Viewing current events through the lens of biblical prophecy, he believed it was evident that soon—very soon—the world would be engulfed in a terror never before imagined. In 2002, he began working on a new book to help make sense out of the confusing events that filled the headlines. From that unfinished work—and his classic *Armageddon, Oil and the Middle East Crisis*—comes *Armageddon, Oil, and Terror.*

John F. Walvoord
Bibliography

Author

The Doctrine of the Holy Spirit

The Holy Spirit

The Return of the Lord

The Thessalonian Epistles

The Rapture Question

The Millennial Kingdom

To Live Is Christ

Israel in Prophecy

The Church in Prophecy

The Revelation of Jesus Christ

The Nations in Prophecy

Jesus Christ Our Lord

Daniel: The Key to Prophetic Revelation

Philippians: Triumph in Christ

The Holy Spirit at Work Today

Matthew: Thy Kingdom Come

The Blessed Hope and the Tribulation

221

The Nations, Israel and the Church in Prophecy

Every Prophecy of the Bible (formerly *The Prophecy Knowledge Handbook*)

What We Believe

Major Bible Prophecies

The Final Drama (formerly *Prophecy*)

End Times

Prophecy in the New Millennium

Coauthor

The Prophetic Word in Crisis Days

Armageddon, Oil and the Middle East Crisis

Five Views on Sanctification

Four Views on Hell

Contributor

Modern Debating

Not by Bread Alone

The Sure Word of Prophecy

Winona Echoes

Light for the World's Darkness

Understanding the Times

The Word for This Century

The Coming World Church

Focus on Prophecy

Fresh Winds of the Holy Spirit

Prophetic Truth Unfolding Today

Prophecy in the Making

Prophecy in the Seventies

Jesus the King Is Coming

Founder's Week Messages

America in History and Bible Prophecy

Money for Ministries

Issues in Dispensationalism

Vital Theological Issues

Vital Prophetic Issues
Raging into Apocalypse
Foreshocks of Antichrist
Vital Christology Issues
Forewarning
The Road to Armageddon
Countdown to Armageddon
Foreshadows of Wrath and Redemption

Editor

Inspiration and Interpretation
Truth for Today: Bibliotheca Sacra Reader
Major Bible Themes (revised)
Chafer's Systematic Theology (abridged)

Coeditor

The Bib Sac Reader
Bible Knowledge Commentary (two volumes)
The Life of Christ Commentary

Mark Hitchcock
Bibliography

Author

Iran: The Coming Crisis

Could the Rapture Happen Today?

55 Answers to Questions about Life after Death

The Truth behind Left Behind (with coauthor Tommy Ice)

End Times Answers Series

   The Four Horsemen of the Apocalypse

   What Jesus Says about Earth's Final Days

   Seven Signs of the End Times

   Is the Antichrist Alive Today?

   The Coming Islamic Invasion of Israel

   Is America in Bible Prophecy?

   What On Earth Is Going On?

The Second Coming of Babylon

101 Answers to the Most Asked Questions about the End Times

The Complete Book of Bible Prophecy

After the Empire: Bible Prophecy in Light of the Fall of the Soviet Union

Contributor

Tim LaHaye Prophecy Study Bible

The Gathering Storm

The End Times Controversy

The Popular Encyclopedia of Bible Prophecy

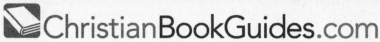